MORRIE:
Only in America

Morris Friedman

Dedication

To my mother and father, brothers Paul and Carl,
and the young people of the land that I love, America

ACKNOWLEDGMENTS

I'd like to thank the people who helped me write this book, including, first and foremost, my son, Steven. He encouraged me to put my ideas into book form and worked with me from start to finish. I'd also like to thank Jay Skolnick for his patience and everlasting true friendship; Joel Miller for his time, input, and willingness to stay with it; Dave Shookman, for being a wealth of information and a very, very good friend; Pat O'Connor for always pushing a project, bringing humor to every situation, and being a friend; Lisa Barrass just for being a friend; and Heather Perry, my tireless secretary. And thank you Geri and Gertrude for all your input.

I would also like to thank the people in the steel industry—a great industry—who made such a lasting and positive impression on my life.

And of course, everlasting thanks to my lovely wife, Phyllis, who always made the greatest impression of all. I love you dearly.

Also, thank you so much, Barry Fox.

TABLE OF CONTENTS

PREFACE

Many years ago, quite likely before you were born, I immigrated to this country as a teenage boy. Coming from a tiny village in Czechoslovakia, a country where persecution and poverty were routine, I was astonished to see people walking on the streets of New York City with their heads held high. To me, everyone seemed to be rich—even the workmen, who wore real shoes!

This was in the 1930s, right in the middle of the terrible Great Depression, yet everywhere in America people were talking about a better tomorrow. I had never heard anything like that where I came from, because just getting through each day was all we hoped for. But here, people were always thinking about possibilities, always dreaming and working and planning to get ahead.

I knew almost nothing about America when I stepped off the ship, other than what I had picked up by looking at pictures in American magazines I couldn't read because I didn't know the language. The only thing I knew for sure was that it was a place where great things were possible.

Within a few years, I learned a great deal about this country, including that the people treasured their flag and what it stood for, believed in democracy and liberty for all, prized a hard day's work, respected those who had achieved much, and were willing to shed their blood to defend their beliefs. America was the place that people all around the world dreamed about because it was the place where dreams could come true.

But that America has been fading away for years. And it's rapidly being replaced by an America filled with people who no longer dream of the great possibilities: people who feel that living on government handouts is perfectly acceptable, who mock our history and flag, who believe that this country is a danger to the world, who look to the government for all the answers, and who no longer believe that great things are possible for this country or its people.

What is happening to this country is absolutely terrifying to me. If it continues, we will become continuously weaker, economically and militarily, and slide into social balkanization, divided into dramatically opposed groups who try to kick each other to the ground even as we hold out our hands to the government to demand more freebies. And as America goes, so goes the world. Without a strong America protecting freedom, democracy, and capitalism, these three blessings will eventually disappear.

That's why I wrote this book: as a reminder of why old-fashioned American beliefs in individual freedom and responsibility are so important. I begin by telling the story of how I came to this country and found ways to succeed. It's not an unusual tale, but I hope it will help you understand what America stood for in days past, before it became fashionable to mock our history and values, before our children were raised with the idea that America must somehow be restrained or the world will suffer terribly.

I tell my story in Part I. Then in Part II, I go on to explain why I believe America is exceptional, why it is so important that we rediscover our commitment to freedom, democracy, and capitalism, and why we must rededicate ourselves to spreading these wonderful gifts across the globe.

This book is my legacy to America, the land that I love. My fondest wish is that our young people will develop a strong and abiding love for our country and its ideals. For without this, our country has no future.

PART I:
MY STORY

CHAPTER ONE

They *Will* Respect Me

One of my earliest memories in life is being awakened early on Friday mornings, hurrying through my breakfast of watery potato soup and a piece of bread, then setting out on foot on the rutted dirt road that connected our tiny village of Vapenik to the rest of the world. The others I passed on my way—farmers in their horse-drawn wagons, peasant women carrying huge bundles of clothing or food, the occasional workman with his farm tools strapped to his back—often laughed at me.

"Look at the little boy," they would say, or "Such a big load for such a small boy." It must have been an amusing sight, a barefoot five-year-old, small for his age, dressed in ragged clothes, closely cropped hair covered by a cloth cap and long *payos* (ear locks) curling down over both cheeks, carrying a live chicken in his arms. Sometimes the chicken, whose legs were tied together, would slip out of my arms and try to hop away, squawking loudly. That also must have been a funny sight, a little boy chasing after a chicken with its legs tied together.

I was on my way to Svidnič́k, a small village two to three kilometers away that was home to three or four Jewish families. That may not sound like many Jews, but it was enough that a *shochet* would be there every Friday to slaughter chickens for that night's dinner, which began *Shabbos* (the Jewish Sabbath). A *shochet* is a man trained in the art of slaughtering animals so the meat can be considered kosher. Arriving in Svidnič̌k, I would hand the chicken to the heavily bearded man and watch as he examined the bird to make sure it was healthy and unblemished. Then he would draw his very sharp knife rapidly across the chicken's throat so the blood would flow out of the chicken's body quickly, as prescribed by the ancient rabbis. After the organs and blood vessels were examined to make sure the slaughter had been properly performed, the now-kosher chicken would be handed back to me.

With my arms wrapped tightly around the dead chicken, I would begin my long journey home. If the weather was cold I would hurry, but when it was warm I took my time, wandering off the road now and then to gaze at horses or cows feeding on the grass, or rest in a shady spot under a tree. There were fields and trees everywhere—as soon as I walked a short distance from any village, all I could see were fields and trees. The trees grew mostly on top of the gently rolling hills, while the fields lay between the hills. During the spring and summer, everything became part of a beautiful mosaic of different shades of green.

Today it would seem crazy to allow a five-year-old to walk a long distance, alone and unprotected, for hours at a time. But back then, where I was from, it was common. The year was 1925, and we lived in a tiny village that was nothing more than twenty-five or thirty houses strung haphazardly along a dirt road that wandered through the hills from one town to another in the eastern half of Czechoslovakia. I never knew the name of the road; it probably had one, but to us it was just "the road." Other than the houses, there was nothing in Vapenik but a little church at one end of town, and in that church there was a little school for the village children. There were no stores, no repair shops, nothing.

Nestled in a little valley with the hills a short distance across the fields on either side of the road, Vapenik was home to two dozen farmers who scraped by year after year working their small plots, rarely making enough money to replace the rags they wore, which had been handed down through the generations. Real shoes were not common: many people in our village wore *buskor*, pieces of leather that were wound around the feet, then wrapped with strips of cloth and string to hold them together. The one time I was given new shoes, when I was eleven or twelve years old, they were made out of paper and fell apart as soon as I "skied" down a small, snow-covered hill near our farm.

We Friedmans were the poorest family in Vapenik because my father was a lousy farmer. He didn't know anything about raising crops or handling animals, and he didn't care. He had only become a farmer because he married my mother, who had inherited a farm from her father. Theirs was an arranged marriage that must have seemed like a great idea at the time. For my mom, Sarah, marrying a learned man who came from a family of rabbis was a big step up. For my father, Aba Zalke, marrying a girl who owned a farm meant he could earn a living while he continued his studies. I guess no one stopped to think that a man who, from an early age, had spent all of his time studying the Torah and other holy writings might not enjoy wrapping his hands around cows' teats or shoveling horse manure.

As for my mom, she didn't have a moment's happiness from the day they were married. Not one. How could she, when she had been forced to make a life with a husband who preferred studying ancient writings to being yoked to a poorly educated farm girl? A man who hardly ever did any work on the farm, but managed to *daven* (pray) every day, smoke cigarettes, drink a lot of coffee, visit friends and relatives, and take the biggest chunk of butter as soon as his wife churned it to give to his sister in a nearby town. When he did work, well, he couldn't drive a nail into a board without smashing his finger. My mother and father simply couldn't understand each other, so they fought and argued all the time, constantly throwing curses at each other in Yiddish and Slovakian.

I adored my mother; she was everything to me. I loved to help her work in our little vegetable garden, and watch her bake bread and churn butter in our little thatched-roof house with its clay floors (only one room had a real wood floor). I loved going out into the fields and woods with her, where she taught me how to distinguish between the safe and dangerous mushrooms by the way they looked. I would go out and pick a bunch of them, then proudly bring them back to her to show her what I had done.

My mother was a beautiful woman who worked very hard to care for my four sisters, three brothers, and me. Every day she got up before the sun and used a sickle to cut grass that she put into a feeder in front of the cows, so they would stand still and eat while she milked them. Then she would tend the vegetables in the garden and dig up potatoes, which she made into soup for our breakfast. Later, she would brush the cows' hides with a special brush and shovel manure out of the barn so the cows could lie down. The rest of the day she worked nonstop. She took care of us children and made our meals. She fertilized the fruit trees and then picked and canned the fruit. I remember how she would cut the pears and other fruit into pieces, setting them out piece by piece on top of the oven so they would dry. She also took care of our horse, helped with the planting and harvesting, and did small repairs around the house and farm—like building fences using the branches of nearby pine trees.

Much of my mother's life was spent in the kitchen, where she baked bread in a large oven, cooked stew and soup over a wood-fired stove, preserved fruit for the winter, mended our clothes, and slept in a little bed in the corner. (Following Orthodox Jewish customs, my father slept elsewhere.) She also spent a lot of time taking care of my sisters' hair. Because of ever-present lice, their long hair had to be washed carefully and then rinsed with a kind of kerosene.

Mom was also our family doctor and knew how to use herbs and even manure as medicines. When we developed sores between our toes, she had us put our feet into the fluid that seeped out of a pile of manure. *Oy!* That burned so much! But soon the sores were healed. One time, while playing with an axe, I nearly split my skull open. Mom stopped the bleeding by packing the wound with bread. Later, she used a mixture of herbs and grass to make a poultice that she put on the wound to disinfect it. It worked beautifully.

My mother was always so busy she had no time to smile. The only times I saw her smile were when I told her stories at night. Unfortunately, this didn't happen very often because, after the age of six, I spent most of my time living in other towns, where I studied Hebrew and the Bible. But when I was home, I would make up stories about the town drunk, exaggerating his slurred speech or his funny way of walking. Those were the only times I ever saw her happy.

Besides being the poorest family in Vapenik, we were the only Jews, which could have put us in a difficult position, as many Czechoslovakians were very anti-Semitic. But years before, when the village church caught fire, my Grandpa Meyer had saved the statue of Mary, and because of that the villagers treated us well. Grandpa was also a very good farmer who always had extra food that he shared with neighbors who were hungry. So even though the other families in the village may have thought we were going to hell because we killed Christ, they were otherwise friendly. In fact, every Christmas, certain villagers enticed me into their homes with an offer of cookies, because it was considered good luck if the first person who walked into your home on Christmas Day was a Jew.

I didn't find out how terrible it was to be a Jew in Czechoslovakia until I left Vapenik and went to *cheder*, a school where Jewish children studied the Torah and other sacred writings and learned Jewish history. This began when I was just six years old, and over the next several years I lived in a succession of nearby towns that were large enough to support a *cheder*. In each town, my father arranged for me to live with distant relatives or even strangers. The first of these towns was Kapishov, which was about five miles away from Vapenik and much bigger than any town I'd ever seen. There were several Jewish families living in

Kapishov because it had a furniture parts factory that hired Jews as accountants and managers. These Kapishov Jews were wealthy compared to us. They wore nice clothes and their houses had wooden roofs and wooden floors in every room. I was impressed by the streets in Kapishov because they also had wooden sidewalks that allowed me to stay above the mud and muck. But it was on those very sidewalks that I first learned how a government can abuse its people. In Kapishov, if a government official was walking down the sidewalk and you happened to be in his way, you had to hop off immediately into the street, even if it meant stepping into muck. That was the way it was in Czechoslovakia back then, and in many other European countries as well: the government officials had all the power, prestige, and money. And everyone else was just in their way.

Being a common person in Czechoslovakia was degrading enough, but being a Jew was much worse. Nobody bothered us in Vapenik, but in the rest of the Slovakian half of the county (the eastern part, where I lived), the majority of people were anti-Semitic. The Czech half (the western part of the country) was different. They were more modern; they lived in bigger cities and were more educated, so they were more tolerant. But in the Slovak half, we Jews were targets. They could tell at a glance that we were Jewish by our clothing and the *payos* hanging down in front of the men's and boys' ears. And they treated us poorly. At train stops, when we were waiting to board, people would push us to the side and take our places. In the stores and on the streets, people made loud comments about us and our "deviant religion," about how

Jews were only interested in money and we were all cheats. As for the young *goys* (non-Jews), they were more than happy to knock us around. Starting when I first went to Kapishov at age six and continuing as I moved to other towns, there were always local bullies eager to tug on my *payos* or knock my cap off. And as I grew older, they did more.

My father was the one who took me to Kapishov; we hitched a ride on a farmer's wagon for a little while, then walked the rest of the way. Once there, we went right to the *cheder*, where I met the skinny, bearded, mean-looking teacher who ran the school. The *cheder* itself was nothing more than a little room with a few tables and chairs and a lot of books. But it would become my "home," the place where I slept alone on the floor on a thin straw mattress in the corner of a cold, dark room and cried myself to sleep every night. As for food, my father arranged for seven Jewish families to feed me, and I would go to a different family's home each evening for dinner. (Each family also sent lunch to the *cheder* for me on their assigned day.) Some families fed me well, but others just gave me a little stale bread and leftovers, so I was often hungry— so hungry that my stomach hurt. My favorite day was Tuesday, because that was the day I went to the home of Mr. Dovid Einhorn, who worked as an accountant in the factory's office. He was a very educated man with beautiful clothes and boots, who always wore aftershave that smelled so good. The Einhorns fed me very well.

Five and a half days a week I studied in the *cheder*. There the teacher taught a small group of children the *aleph-bes* (Hebrew alphabet) and recounted the stories of Moses, King David, and other biblical heroes. We were taught to chant prayers such as the *Shema Yisrael*, to cherish our heritage, and become good members of the Jewish community.

I hated *cheder*. My parents had not taught me how to pray or read Hebrew at home, so I was far behind the other students before school even began. It was tough for me to pay attention, and the teacher often smacked me with a ruler when I gave the wrong answer.

"Such a *goyishe kopf*!" he would say, which meant I wasn't thinking like a Jew.

Maybe I was such a bad student because I was often hungry and didn't care much about some God I didn't understand. Or maybe it was because I missed my mother so much it hurt and I felt so alone. In Kapishov, I was nothing, just a little Jew whom the *goys* disliked. The Jews in Kapishov also looked down on me, considering me a "country Jew," a bumpkin who lacked manners and couldn't possibly be smart. Even the teacher treated me like I was less than the other children, who all came from town, not the farm.

Three times every *shabbos*—on Friday night, Saturday morning and Saturday evening—I accompanied the teacher to the room next door to the *cheder*, where the Jewish men gathered to pray. They all wore their best coats with beautiful buttons, and hung their coats on hooks in the foyer. Then one night, while they were praying, someone cut off all of those buttons. Naturally, they immediately blamed me, the mischievous little country Jew who liked to tie other boy's shoelaces to the furniture legs and do naughty things like that. The men all scolded me for something I hadn't done, which was very painful. Only Mr. Einkorn, the one who always fed me well, refrained.

Then, a few days later, Mr. Einhorn called me over and said, "Moishe, just tell me. Did you do it?"

I replied, "I never even *looked* at those coats."

He nodded as he considered my answer for a moment. Then he said, "I believe you," and that was the end of that. No one ever mentioned it again.

I went to the Kapishov *cheder* for a few years and learned a few things, but mostly I daydreamed about my next visit home, when I would help my mother in the garden, ride our horse, and play with my brothers and sisters. I also dreamed about a place called America, where my mother's brothers, Uncle Jack and Uncle Herman, and her father, Grandpa Meyer, had gone to live. I couldn't explain where America was, or say anything about it other than it was a wonderful place where anyone could succeed. But I knew this for a fact, because we would get packages from Grandpa Meyer containing clothes that were new and beautiful to us, even though they had already been worn by the family. There were also toys and shiny yellow pencils that had "Builder's Structural Steel" stamped on the side. That was the name of my uncles' company, which was in a place called Cleveland, where Jews were not persecuted and could make so much money they could afford to send five-dollar and ten-dollar bills in the mail. Five dollars was a fortune to us—it would feed us for weeks! And my grandpa was adding five- and ten-dollar bills to our packages like they were pennies!

By the time I was seven or eight years old, I knew exactly what I wanted to do in life. I wanted to go to America, make a lot of money, and take care of my mother. I would make sure she always had fancy white flour for baking, a new dress every year, and a wonderful life. These things would make her very happy.

But in the meantime, I continued studying in *cheder*. In Stropkov, a city some sixteen miles from Vapenik where I went to regular Czechoslovakian school during the day and then *cheder* afterwards, I lived with the Laner family, all of whom were very kind to me. For once I had a real bed to sleep on! The Laners owned a bakery, and they taught me to bake bread, which I delivered to their customers in the afternoons after *cheder*. I loved the Laners but only got to stay with them a little while before being sent to a town called Košice, where I lived with the Guttmans, who were my mother's relatives. They were also nice, but no matter how nice a family was to me, even if they fed me well, I just wanted to go back to Vapenik. I really wanted to be at home with my mother and my family.

When I was twelve, my father sent me to Sbrovof to live with another second cousin, where I was to prepare for my bar mitzvah. Unlike the towns I'd lived in before, Sbrovof was a real city with paved streets and buildings that were two or more stories high. But I didn't like it there. Although I had a place to sleep at my cousin's house, it was just a blanket laid out on a board on the floor. And I still had to go from house to house to get my meals.

My days were spent attending public school, going to *cheder* in the afternoon after school was out, finding my way to the family that would feed me that night, and returning to my cousin's house to sleep on the floor.

That would have been bad enough. But what I really detested was the tall, blond *shegetz* (non-Jewish male) who used to wait for me to leave *cheder* in the late afternoons. His name was Vasil, and he never lost an opportunity to remind me that I was born inferior. He would suddenly appear across the street as I left *cheder* and scream, "Hey, little Jew!" or "Christ killer!" Then he would march across the street like he owned it and grab me by my *payos*. He would pull my head downward, and once he got me into a stooping position, suddenly thrust his hands into the air, snapping my head up and pulling so hard on my *payos* I thought the sides of my head would come off.

If I was lucky, he would have a good laugh and then walk away, hurling a few more insults as he went. But if I wasn't so lucky, I would wind up on the ground being kicked to remind me that I was subhuman. It never occurred to me to fight back, because I was very small and skinny for my age and had no idea how to fight. More importantly, I had no idea that I deserved to stand up for myself. Instead, I tried tucking my *payos* behind my ears before leaving *cheder*. But, of course, that didn't do me any good. Vasil knew I was a Jew with no protection, so I was fair game.

One day, I was walking back to my cousin's house from *cheder* when Vasil made another grinning appearance. By this time, I'd had enough. All of the kids who went to *cheder* had been given a large skeleton key to the building. I reached into my pocket and grabbed that key, wrapping my palm around it and letting its pronged end protrude from between my knuckles.

When Vasil started in with his insults, I shouted back, "If you cross that street and try to hit me, I'll put holes in your head!"

"You fucking little Jew! I'll kill you!" he snarled, as he charged across the street.

There was no way I was backing down this time. I didn't care if he killed me; I wasn't going to give a single inch. Just as Vasil was about to pounce on me, I pulled my fist out of my pocket, swung hard, and slammed the end of the key right into the middle of his forehead!

Stunned and bleeding, Vasil staggered backward, holding his forehead and screaming, "Help me! Help me! The Jew-boy hit me!"

Immediately the street seemed to fill with people and I raced off, sure that I would be arrested. Where we lived, if a Jew hit a *goy*, everyone would automatically believe that the Jew was at fault.

Sure enough, the police came to see me at my cousin's house to make a report of the incident, but nothing much came of it— nothing much except that I was evicted from my cousin's house. And when my father came to fetch me, he hit me with a belt a few times. But to me, these things were nothing. What was important, what was *everything*, was I had finally stood up to that bully. It felt great—and *I* felt great! I knew that from then on, no bully would wrestle me to the ground again. People were going to respect me. They might not love me, they might not even like me, but they would *respect* me. Of that, I was sure.

CHAPTER TWO

Coming "Home" to America

Shortly after my bar mitzvah, I cut off my *payos*, which made my father go berserk. You have to understand, wearing *payos* isn't just a fashion among religious Jews: it's a commandment that comes from a passage in Leviticus that says you shall not cut the "corners" of your hair. Taking it one step further, Maimonides, one of the greatest of all Jewish scholars, insisted that only heathens shave off their ear locks. But I didn't care. Not only did I cut my *payos*, I began to let my hair grow. I knew a Jewish man in Svidnick, a guy who was maybe thirty years old, who had cut off his *payos* and beard and let his hair grow. We met because he ran a beer garden not far from where my older brother worked in a clothing store. One time he said to me, "Hey, kid, you want a ride on my motorcycle?" I jumped at the chance, got behind him on the seat, and held on tight as we raced up and down the roads. It was thrilling to go so fast! I felt like I was king of the hill! Maybe I thought cutting my *payos* and growing my hair would make me more like him: powerful, independent, and carefree.

"It's a *shanda*!" my red-faced father shouted when he first saw me with no *payos*. A *shanda* is a disgrace that is so bad it shames the entire family. In his eyes, not only was cutting off my *payos* a disgrace, it was a blatant rejection of our heritage and everything he stood for. But to me, wearing *payos* marked me as a lesser person, and I didn't want to have anything to do with that kind of heritage. I couldn't stand being automatically considered less than everyone else.

As for rejecting my father, in truth the two of us had no relationship, so there was nothing to reject. We weren't antagonistic: we just went our own ways until I did something he thought was wrong, like hitting a bully in the head. Then he felt he had to punish me. Unfortunately, I was always doing something wrong, like the time I snatched a neighbor's accordion from his front porch and took it home so I could learn to play it. Or ate non-kosher food at the home of another villager. Every time I did something like this, my father would say to my mom, "Who does he take after, the little devil?" She never replied.

I didn't know who I took after, but it wasn't him. Perhaps I shouldn't judge him, because I was only able to view him through a child's eyes; the last time I saw him I was only fifteen and a half years old. But it was clear to me, even then, that he was a man who was out of place, a Biblical scholar from generations of learned men who had ended up stuck on a farm. Maybe he was ashamed of being a poor farmer, one who had to accept gifts of money and clothing from his rich in-laws in America and beg for handouts from his own family. When he took me to different towns to drop me off for school or *cheder*, he always visited certain people who gave him money. When we went to Stropkov, for example, he would always visit a young man named Henry Moskowitz, who would later marry my sister Evelyn. Henry sold horses, and my father would say things to him like, "Did that guy come to see you?

The one I sent over to buy a horse from you? I told him you had the best horses!" Of course, Dad had never sent anyone to buy anything from him, but big-hearted Henry would play along and give him 20 or 25 kroner as a "commission."

As I look back on the *payos*-cutting incident, I realize that my father was right: I was rejecting everything he stood for, as I understood it. But Judaism meant very different things to the two of us. To him, it was something wonderful, inspiring, and soul-satisfying. But to me, it just meant being poor, kicked around, and forced to accept a certain way of life just because that's the way things were always done. I was tired of dressing in rags with patches on my hind end and being hungry most of the time. I wanted to be strong, free, and able to earn enough money to wear new clothes and fill my belly every day. I wanted to be able to make my own decisions, like my uncles in America.

Even though I had never met them, I admired my Uncles Jack and Herman from afar. In my mind, they were so rich they must have owned half of America! They had gone to America with fifteen cents in their pockets and, from scratch, built their own company, Builder's Structural Steel. That name, embossed on the sides of those yellow pencils they sent us, represented a world of possibilities just waiting for me in the wonderful country called America. Even as a young child I wanted to go there so badly. I used to roll those yellow pencils between my palms and dream about going there and having enough to eat.

Much of what I knew about America came from the movies. Every so often, someone would set up a tent in a field on the edge of town and show American films—talkies with Czech subtitles. I could never afford to buy a ticket, but once it got crowded inside the tent, I could sneak around the side and crawl under the edge of the tent. Then I'd sit right next to a family as if I belonged to them and watch the movies. The family usually knew what I was doing and didn't care. In fact, sometimes they helped: when the man came by checking to see if anyone had sneaked in, the father or mother would put an arm around me as if I was their own child. And that's how I got to see American movies. There were gangster movies, Westerns with Tom Mix and Hoot Gibson and other cowboys, and other kinds of films. I couldn't understand any of the English words, but they sounded magical to me.

One time, when I was about twelve years old, I saw men driving pegs into the ground for a movie tent in a field. I hurried over and helped them put up the tent and set up the chairs, hoping they would give me a free ticket. But that didn't happen, so I had to sneak in. Then, the next day when they were taking the tent down, I told the man in charge that I loved one of the pictures of Tom Mix in the display case; he was riding a horse and looked like he was going a hundred miles an hour! He smiled at me and then gave me the picture—what a prize! Back home in Vapenik a few weeks later, I put the picture in a special hiding place in the wall behind my bed. Some of the boards there were so loose that if you pulled a certain way they would come out. I hid pictures taken from magazines, movie posters, and some other things there. One day, when I was away at *cheder*, my father pulled my bed out to make some repairs on the wall. He found the pictures, and was so mad that his son had these foolish things that he ripped them all into tiny pieces.

Magazines were an important source of information about America for me. At home when I had some free time, I would climb into the loft in the barn where the hay was stored and where I hid my American magazines. They weren't really mine; I would take them from the barber shop or anywhere else I found them, tuck them under my coat, and walk right out. And sometimes Mr. Einhorn gave me some. I never knew the names of these magazines because I couldn't read English. But I loved turning the pages and seeing pictures of big modern buildings in huge lit-up cities, and beautiful houses perched on cliffs above the ocean. I also loved looking at pictures of people wearing fancy clothing and driving shiny new cars.

From a very early age I knew that I would go to America one day. But in the meantime, I had to keep going to Czechoslovakian school and working. By working, I mean serving as an apprentice baker, first with the Laners and then with the Guttmans. Although everyone was nice to me, I didn't want to be a baker. The worst part was that I had to start work every day at midnight, kneading the dough, forming it into loaves, rolls, and other shapes, putting caraway seeds on top of the loaves, then sliding everything into the ovens to bake. I was so small, I had to stand on a little stool to do my work. When all was ready hours later, I would put the fresh hot loaves into a special basket with straps that went over my shoulders, hop on a bicycle and pedal through the town, dropping different kinds of bread off at different houses. Once this was done, I went back to the bakery and had breakfast with the family. That was nice; we would laugh a lot. After breakfast I slept a little, then went to Czechoslovakian school. In exchange for being an apprentice, I was given room and board and, once in a while, a little bit of money that I could use to buy shoes or something else I needed.

One of the things I spent my money on was a little cart with wheels that I used to haul packages and suitcases for people who came in at the bus station. I only did this on Saturdays, because that was the day the bakery was closed. And if cutting off my *payos* was a *shanda*, this was even worse, because Saturday is the Jewish Sabbath, when it is forbidden to work. You're not supposed to do any kind of work at all, but there I was, stacking packages and suitcases on my cart and *schlepping* them all over town. When my customers gave me a few coins, I committed yet another sin, because you're not supposed to handle money on the Sabbath. I thought nobody in my family would ever know because I was in a town miles away from Vapenik, but someone who knew me saw what I was doing and word soon got around. When my mother found out what I was doing, she was heartbroken. But I had a very good reason. "I just wanted to make enough money to buy you some white flour," I told her. White flour was a real delicacy in Vapenik, where the flour was brown and coarse and produced dense, chewy baked goods. My mom deserved to have white flour.

By the beginning of 1936, when I was fifteen years old, everyone was talking about Hitler and what was happening to the Jews in Germany. My parents became very worried and wrote to Grandpa Meyer in America to ask if he would help the family emigrate. Grandpa Meyer then spoke to his son, my Uncle Jack, who agreed to help, and they decided that the children should be sent over first, a few at a time, and the parents would come last. Since my parents knew I was crazy about America and was approaching draft age in Czechoslovakia, they decided I would go first, along with my twenty-year-old sister Evelyn, who was old enough to serve as my guardian on the ship to America.

I knew this was the plan but had no idea when it would happen. So I was surprised when, while working at Guttman's bakery one day, I got a message telling me to meet my father and sister at the train station on a certain date: Evelyn and I were going to America! I was so excited that all I could think about was going to America.

On the appointed day, I met my father and sister, and we took the train to Prague to get our visas from the American embassy. We checked into a hotel and went straightaway to the embassy, where my sister and I were examined by doctors. Then we waited for a long time before we were taken, one at a time, into a room where a handsome, important-looking man in a herringbone suit sat behind a big mahogany desk. I was particularly impressed by his wide shirt cuffs and colorful tie.

Evelyn went in first to be questioned by the man. Somebody, perhaps Uncle Jack, must have already made most of the arrangements, for the forms on the man's desk were almost completely filled out. Evelyn told me that the man asked her some routine questions through an interpreter, then asked: "What are you going to do in America?"

Without thinking, she replied, "Marry my uncle."

She had some idea that she might marry Uncle Herman, who was a bachelor.

Boom! The man stamped her papers with the "Rejected" stamp, and that was that. She wasn't going anywhere but back to Vapenik.

When it was my turn, he asked some questions, then said, "What are you going to do in America?"

"How do I know?" I replied honestly. "I'm not there yet."

His face lit up with a smile, and he stamped my papers with the "Accepted" stamp.

Evelyn was so angry that she didn't get her visa, she complained all the way back to the hotel. That night, as my father and I were settling into the bed we were sharing, he said to me sadly, "Moishe, you're going to forget about us." Even in the dim light I could see a tear on his cheek. It was the first time I ever saw him cry.

I replied, "*Tateh*," which means "father." "I'll never forget you."

I tried to say it like I meant it, but I really wasn't thinking about whether I would ever see him again. I was only thinking about America.

The truth is, I couldn't wait to get out of Czechoslovakia, and was afraid that the man from the Embassy would change his mind and take away my visa. So instead of going back home with my father and Evelyn to say goodbye to my mother, I got on a train to France and waved at the two of them through a window as we pulled out of the station. I was on my way to Cherbourg, a beautiful seaside town on the northwestern tip of France just across the channel from England. And once there, I would board the ship that would take me to America. I was fifteen and a half and felt that my life was finally beginning.

In order to get to France from Prague, we had to go straight through Germany, which was quite frightening. We had all heard about that *mamzer* (bastard) Hitler and the brutal Nazi party. Stories were going around about how the Nazis had stripped the German Jews of their citizenship, banned them from being doctors or other professionals, set up boycotts of Jewish shops, and persecuted the Jews in countless other ways. We had also heard about Jews who were beaten just for being Jewish. As I sat on a train that became increasingly filled with Nazis and traveled straight through Germany, I was extremely glad I had cut my *payos* off years before. If any of the Nazis sitting nearby had known they were traveling with a Jew, I could easily have been in trouble.

Once the train arrived in Cherbourg, those of us going to the docks were ushered onto buses. And when the ship came into view, I could hardly believe my eyes. It was enormous; from the waterline it rose higher than any building I had ever seen. And at the very top, four huge smokestacks soared even higher. This wasn't just any old ship but the *Aquitania*, part of the famous Cunard White Star Line. I was so excited I could hardly stand still. For a country boy who had never seen any kind of seagoing vessel before, not even a rowboat, this gigantic ship with ten decks stacked on top of each other was an incredible sight. There were so many portholes dotting the side of the ship, I couldn't count them all! Somebody later told me the ship could hold 2,200 passengers, a fact that would have been beyond my comprehension when I first laid eyes on it. I had never even seen 2,200 people in one place, much less crowded onto one massive, fantastic ship.

But right away there was a problem. Because I was a minor child, I wasn't allowed to go aboard by myself. The plan had been that Evelyn would sign for me but obviously she wasn't there. For a few heart-stopping moments I could imagine myself being sent back to Czechoslovakia and getting stuck there for years until I got another chance to leave.

Fortunately, the blue-suited agent for the Cunard Line seemed to know exactly what to do when I handed him my passport and other papers. It even seemed that he had been waiting for me.

"Come with me," he said briskly, leading me over to a nicely dressed couple. I assumed they were Americans because they spoke English and were on their way to New York.

"This is the boy," the agent said.

They looked surprised. "He's fifteen?!" the man asked. I suppose they couldn't imagine that someone so small and skinny could be that old.

The agent checked my visa. "Yes. Fifteen and a half."

The nicely dressed couple shrugged, signed some papers that said they were acting as my guardians, then walked off without me. They went up to first class and I headed down to the bowels of the ship, right at the water line, where third-class passengers like me were supposed to stay. We knew that we had to stay there because the ship's translators announced this in different languages several times to make sure everyone understood.

When at long last we were underway, I was amazed at how much movement there was; the floor rose and fell and the walls rocked back and forth like trees in the wind. It was fun for the first few minutes, but before long I got so seasick I thought I was going to die. For the next three days I did nothing but lie on my bunk. And then, miraculously, I started to feel better and was able to begin exploring the ship, wandering through the areas where third-class passengers were allowed to go. In some places, you could peer around a pillar and see beautifully dressed people walking on the decks or sitting in nice chairs. Once, I wandered into a nice part of the ship by mistake, and saw people eating at tables loaded with fancy-looking food. I wanted to be on *that* part of the ship! But I only stood there for a few moments before one of the stewards escorted me back to the bowels of the ship where I belonged.

And then, finally, the great day arrived and our ship pulled into New York harbor. I stood on a jam-packed deck, jumping as high as I could to try to see over the heads of others and catch the first glimpses of the Statue of Liberty lifting her lamp into the sky. As we moved into the harbor and approached Ellis Island, she got bigger and more beautiful every moment. Even though my entire family and all of my friends were back in Czechoslovakia, when we docked in New York harbor I felt like I had come home.

Those of us in third class had to wait a long time for the first- and second-class passengers to disembark. And once we finally walked down the gangplank, they herded us into a building with a gigantic hall that could have held fifty of the houses we had back in Vapenik. The man and woman who had signed for me back in

Cherbourg were supposed to have told the authorities about me, but they forgot and were long gone. I waited and waited and after a while almost all the other passengers had gone. I started to get scared: I didn't know the language; I didn't know who was coming for me and I had no idea what to do if I was forgotten. And I was very afraid that the authorities were going to send me back.

I sat there all alone in that big room for the rest of the day, getting hungrier and hungrier. At last, one of the officials took pity on me and gave me a half pint of milk. I was stunned: I had never had that much milk to drink in one sitting! Then someone else handed me a sandwich, which was a completely foreign object to me. I couldn't understand why anyone would put meat between two pieces of bread. I actually had to be shown how to eat it! But I wasn't embarrassed. I was just happy to have so much food—and for free. I was so excited, I started bouncing up and down while the agents laughed at me. "What a great place America is!" I thought.

Finally, someone came to pick me up. But it wasn't my Uncle Jack or Uncle Herman, the ones who owned Builder's Structural Steel. It was my mother's brother-in-law, Uncle Harry Schonwetter, who had spent the day looking for me in the immigration office. It took until 5:00 p.m. before everything got straightened out. Uncle Harry had been looking for two people, a young woman and a teenage boy, not just one young-looking, impossibly skinny boy. This, coupled with the fact that Uncle Harry had no idea what I looked like, made for major delays in figuring things out and signing the proper papers. But when everything was settled and I walked out of the building holding Uncle Harry's hand, everything was suddenly fine. In fact, everything was *wonderful*. I felt reborn.

It took a couple of months before Evelyn, my three other sisters and my older brother Erwin made it to the United States. But I never saw my mother and father again, or my two younger brothers, because they were all murdered during the Holocaust. To my everlasting regret, I never said goodbye to my mother.

CHAPTER THREE

Where's the Banana Tree?

From the time Uncle Harry took me by the hand until we arrived at his apartment in the Bronx, I couldn't stop staring: at the impossibly tall buildings, which made those three- and four-story buildings I had seen in Prague and Cherbourg look short and squat. And at the thousands of cars and taxis and buses crowding the street. Back home in Vapenik, no one had ever even seen a car. When I would come back from Svidnick or one of the other little towns where I'd been living, the people in Vapenik, most of whom had never once left our little village, would ask me, "Did you see a car?" If I said "yes," they would get very excited and ask me what it looked like. But in New York, there were so many cars it was hard to focus on just one.

To me, the most fascinating part of the big city was the people. I saw men in broad-shouldered, double-breasted business suits made of very nice fabrics, with women on their arms dressed in tight-fitting jackets with tiny waists and padded shoulders, just like in the magazine ads. Even the workmen wore real shoes and decent-looking overalls that were *not* covered with patches! With all of these beautiful buildings, cars, and clothes on literally every corner, it seemed to me that everyone in America must be a millionaire.

While I was staring at these fantastic sights, Uncle Harry continually talked to me in Yiddish, the language of the Jews of eastern and northern Europe, interspersed with English.

"Listen," he would say, "*Vi iz der mishpokhe?*" which means "How is the family?"

Or "Listen, *vi iz dayn mamen?*" That means, "How is your mother?"

This was very puzzling. Finally I asked, in Yiddish, "Who is this guy 'Listen' you're talking to?"

The first thing Uncle Harry did, I'm very glad to say, was take me to a men's clothing store, where he bought me a suit. I had never had a suit before and, in fact, had never had *any* clothing that was brand new. The suit was gray with beautifully cuffed pants—I had never seen cuffs on pants before—and he also bought me a gorgeous blue shirt. I couldn't believe I was being given such a wonderful gift.

Once I had my new suit, we made our way to Uncle Harry's store, an Italian grocery named Harry's sitting in the middle of an Italian neighborhood in the Bronx. The whole family, including my Aunt Rose (my mother's sister) and my cousins Gertrude and Albert, lived in an apartment above the store, but they were waiting for me downstairs. As soon as I walked in, Aunt Rose ran over and hugged me like I was her own son. She told me she remembered me from Czechoslovakia, because she had lived with us for a while in Vapenik when I was very little, before Uncle Harry sent for her from America.

She cried, "My little Moishe!" When she had last seen me, I was only about five years old. My two cousins greeted me very nicely, although they were not sure what to make of this stranger from Europe suddenly showing up. Then we went upstairs to the apartment, where Aunt Rose fed me a bigger meal than I had ever had in my life, and afterwards showed me to my very own bedroom.

The next morning after breakfast, I was sent downstairs to the store and put to work. Running an Italian grocery might seem like an odd business for a Jewish family, but during World War I, Harry, who was from Poland, had fought for the Austrian army and had been captured by Italy. While he was languishing in the prisoner-of-war camp, he learned Italian. So a few years later, when he moved to the United States and was ready to go into business for himself, it seemed natural for him to open an Italian grocery. He could easily speak to his customers and already knew something about Italian food.

The store was maybe 30 feet wide and 120 feet long, with long rows of shelves stocked with canned and dry goods. There was also a meat counter, where Uncle Harry offered his customers sliced Italian ham, Italian salami, and other kinds of meat, plus a cheese counter with big wheels of delicious-smelling aged cheese. Right away, Uncle Harry set me to work unpacking boxes, hauling food from the storeroom, stocking the shelves, and so on. It was very busy that day because it happened to be a Saturday, the day the Italians bought the food they would need for Sunday dinner. I couldn't believe how many people were coming and going through that front door. I also thought it was a little strange that we were working on the Sabbath, but Uncle Harry said we needed to be open on the busiest day of the week, and in that neighborhood it happened to be Saturday.

During the afternoon of that first day, eager to learn as much as I could as fast as I could, I asked Uncle Harry to teach me how to count American money. I didn't know the first thing about nickels, dimes, and quarters, so he patiently laid out the coins, explained their value and showed me how to make change from dollar bills. I caught on fast and before the end of the day, he was letting me run the cash register. I also had to learn very quickly about American pounds and ounces because, as in all grocery stores, certain goods were priced according to weight. It was a little confusing at first, because in Czechoslovakia we always used grams and kilos, but I soon got the hang of it. From then on, I worked in the store every morning and evening and loved every minute of it.

Almost as soon as I arrived, Uncle Harry began teaching me Italian so I would be able to speak to the customers and, more importantly, count in their language—*uno, due, tre,* and so on. At the same time, I was learning "one, "two," and "three" in English, and trying to absorb two languages at the same time could get confusing.

As it turned out, I wasn't the only one who was confused. One day, Uncle Harry had me set up a sale table outside the store with cans of whatever we were featuring stacked up like a pyramid: five on the bottom, four in the next row, then three, two, and one on top. When I finished, I stood back and admired my handiwork, then put up a little sign that announced the price: "*Due venti-cinque,*" which means two for twenty-five cents.

Right away, an Italian lady came up and asked me, "*Quanto?*" which means, "How much?"

I pointed to the sign and said, "*Due venti-cinque.*"

She seemed horrified at the price and shot back, in English, "*How* much?"

"*Due venti-cinque.*"

"No," she insisted. "Fifteen cents apiece. I buy two."

"*Due venti-cinque,*" I said, pointing to the sign again and trying my best to be clear. Two for twenty-five cents.

"Fifteen cents apiece; I buy two!" she insisted.

I thought for a split second, then shouted, "Sold!" in English, and handed her the two items for a nickel more than the posted sale price.

Later, I told my uncle what had happened. "I told her '*due venti-cinque*' three times," I explained to him in Yiddish. "I don't speak much Italian or English, so what could I do? I know the word 'sold,' so I said 'sold' and took her money!"

Uncle Harry just smiled, shook his head and asked me who the lady was. When I described her, he nodded and said, "Oh, I know her. She drinks and gets confused." Then he put a mark by the woman's name on his account page.

"What are you doing?"

"I'm making a note so I can tell her husband what happened and give back the extra money."

"Why? She *wanted* to pay thirty cents. Why give it back?"

"Listen, Moishe. I've been doing business with these people for years. When her husband comes in to cash his paycheck and pay his account, we smoke cigars together. I don't want to take even an extra nickel from them, because relationships are very important in business."

It was a good lesson for me.

Working inside the store wasn't my only job. On weekends, I loaded up a pushcart with grocery orders and wheeled it through the streets of the Bronx, delivering food to those who had ordered it. I'd push the cart up this street and down that one, then carry the bags upstairs, sometimes four or five flights. (Nobody had an elevator in those days.) Once I'd dropped off the food, some of the customers would give me a little money as a tip, while others might give me a cup of coffee.

In the beginning, I had a hell of a time finding my way around such a strange and complicated city. And if Aunt Rose didn't spell the street name for me exactly as it appeared on the signs, I would get lost, which happened a lot. I was from a part of the world where most villages had just one road and a total population of fifty or sixty people. Back in the old country, our definition of a "big city" was a place with maybe ten streets and a thousand people. But in the Bronx, there could be a thousand people living in just a two-block area! And in Manhattan, of course, it was even crazier.

After I'd been living in America for a while, I developed a burning desire to see the fantastic Empire State Building, which was only five or six years old at the time and the tallest building in the world. This, of course, required a trip into Manhattan, the heart of New York City, one of the biggest, busiest, and richest cities in the world. I had no idea how to get there, so my cousin Gertrude wrote out some instructions for me. Walk to this place, take a train to that place, transfer to this subway to get to Central Park, take a different subway to another stop and walk a few blocks.

"You'll end up at the entrance to the Empire State Building," Gertrude assured me, "and from the top of the building you can look through a telescope and see for miles." It sounded great, but I had no idea what she was talking about: I'd never heard of a telescope!

The idea of following all of those crazy instructions and making my way through the busy streets of Manhattan was terrifying. Carrying a chicken down a country road for hours was one thing; it was impossible to get lost. But in New York City, one wrong turn and you're finished. As it turned out, I did take a wrong turn and ended up I don't know where. I never did see Central Park or the Empire State Building or any other famous place. Instead, I found myself in a neighborhood with lots of big buildings and store windows displaying men's suits, shirts, and hats. Most of the stores I saw displaying clothing were big, like department stores. But some were quite small, and I wondered how the little ones could possibly sell enough to compete with the big ones and stay in business. I didn't realize that these little stores were the exclusive ones, and selling just one suit would be enough to keep them in business for a while.

I wandered into a few of the bigger stores, fascinated by all of the fancy clothes—what beautiful fabrics, and so many different styles! But in every case, a clerk would hurry up to me and start talking. I thought I knew a lot of English, but it was clear that I knew nothing because I didn't understand anything they said. I always just smiled and nodded, turned and left in a hurry, which I'm sure was what they wanted.

During the first couple of weeks that I worked as a delivery boy, the mothers and grandmothers in every home I visited would come out of their kitchens or back bedrooms to look at me, smile, and feel my bony shoulders. They would talk to each other in Italian and laugh, and their children would come over to me and take a good look. It was obvious they couldn't believe anyone was so skinny.

"*Europa!*" the mothers would say to their children, pointing to me as an example of how bad things were in the old country.

Once I got my bearings, I really enjoyed my delivery job because I got to go outside, explore the neighborhood, and meet people. One of the parts I liked best was visiting a young girl named Rosemary on my route. Oh, was she beautiful! Not only that, she always smiled at me and talked to me when I made deliveries to her family's apartment. I started hanging around awhile when I brought her family's order; we would sit on the porch, talk, and have some coffee and maybe an apple. A couple of times, I actually called her on the telephone. Our phone conversations were short because I didn't speak much English or Italian, but I loved calling her. Then one day, her father came to the store, shoved a finger in my uncle's face and said, "You tell your nephew that if he ever gets too close to my daughter, I'll cut his nuts off!" That was the end of my first romance.

There was so much about America that was new and strange to me, but one thing that truly amazed me was the floors. They were so clean, cleaner than some table tops back home. And I had never seen so much food in all my life! Aunt Rose made wonderful spaghetti, a dish we didn't have in Czechoslovakia, with a thick, meaty tomato sauce that was so delicious I often ate so much I got sick. Meat seemed to be everywhere, which was not the case back home. Before coming to America, I had never even seen a steak, or stews that had more than a tiny amount of meat in them. But these things were fairly common in my new home.

One time, to my surprise, Aunt Rose brought home a bunch of bananas. These were very rare treats in Czechoslovakia and so expensive we could never afford to buy even one. But she had a bunch of six or eight! I couldn't imagine anyone buying so many bananas, even Rockefeller. So I asked her, "Where's the banana tree?" I thought she had to be growing them somewhere.

One thing I could never get used to was that there was so much food that people felt free to throw it away. One time, I saw Aunt Rose tossing loaves of bread in the trash cans behind the store. When she went back into the house, I took a look into the trash can to see what she thought was garbage: the bread was a little old, but it looked fine to me. So I fished it out of the trash, took it upstairs to the apartment, showed it to my aunt and asked, "Why are you throwing this away? We can eat it."

"Oh, my little son," she said, smiling fondly at me. "Here in America, there is enough bread for everyone."

The message was clear: In this country, if a loaf of bread is the least bit stale, you can throw it away because there is plenty more.

You know what else amazed me? Socks! In America, people changed their socks every day, something I had never heard of. At home, we wore our socks for three or four days, rinsed them out and wore them again and again until they had holes in them. Then my mother would darn them. I never wore a pair of socks that weren't all patched up. But once I came to America, I wore a nice clean pair of socks every day.

One of the first things I really wanted to do was to meet Tom Mix and the other cowboys I had seen in the movies. I had dreams of becoming a cowboy myself, and was such a greenhorn that I thought they just walked down the street like everyone else. I made friends with a nice-looking guy named Tony Russo, who was also crazy about cowboys and Tom Mix, and the two of us hung around together after work and talked about getting into the movies. I told him how I'd seen a Tom Mix movie back home when I was fourteen, and after that I practiced jumping on and off our horse, Lissie, like the cowboys in the movie. I'd ride Lissie up and down our property, pushing her to go faster and faster. Then, while she was galloping, I would jump off, touch my feet to the ground while still holding on, then jump right back on her back, just like they did in the movies. Unfortunately, our homemade saddle didn't have a pommel, so I had to grab Lissie's mane. The poor horse was getting on in years and probably not too thrilled with my silliness. But I kept at it anyway, jumping off and on Lissie's back while urging her to go faster and faster.

"So let me guess," Tony said, amused at the thought of my Tom Mix moves. "You ended up falling on your head, right?"

"On my ass!" I said. "So hard I thought I broke it!" We had a good laugh over that one.

I really wanted to become an American: to talk like one, look like one, think like one—and to be in business like one. So I was very happy when Uncle Harry began to give me more duties in the store after just a couple of months. His asthma was getting worse and he needed more rest, so instead of getting up early every morning to open the store, he trained me to do it. He also gave me a rundown on each of his regular customers, so I would know which ones were allowed to get credit and which ones weren't.

I loved being "in charge" in the mornings, unpacking boxes in the back and putting food on the shelves out front, setting up the displays and talking with the customers. I found it fun to argue with the deliverymen when the merchandise they brought was not right and to make them take it back. Uncle Harry had taught me how to cut into the big wheels of cheese that the deliverymen brought and take samples to see if they contained just the right amount of oil. If they didn't, I wouldn't accept them.

Just before lunch, Uncle Harry would come downstairs and I'd tell him what had happened during the morning. Although I did plenty of things wrong because I didn't always understand the language and the culture, he never got upset with me. He just explained how to do better next time.

With the country in the midst of the Great Depression, millions of men were working for the WPA (Works Progress

Administration), constructing roads, dams and buildings. As long as you were willing to work, you could get a job. Once a month, the men who worked for the WPA would come in to the store with their paychecks and give them to Uncle Harry. He would look through his account book to see how much their families had charged during the month, deduct that amount, and give the men the difference in cash. Coming from a country where people without jobs were given no help, I was amazed.

I had been living in America for about a year when my Uncle Jack, one of the two brothers who owned Builder's Structural Steel Company (and all of those wonderful pencils), sent word that he wanted me to move to Cleveland "to work in the family business." This was very exciting news—at long last, I would get to meet my wealthy relatives, Uncle Jack and Uncle Herman! I would have a new job and a new life! But, of course, I would have to leave Uncle Harry, Aunt Rose, and their children, and that was sad. They had been very kind to me and treated me like a member of their family. I was also sorry to say goodbye to my friend Tony Russo. But Uncle Jack was calling me, and I was eager to meet the man who owned a big business and was so rich. So I packed my small bag, said farewell to my wonderful aunt, uncle and cousins, and took off in search of my new life.

CHAPTER FOUR

A Language Sandwich, Please

Back in 1937, when I took my first trip from New York City to Cleveland, the big interstate highways had yet to be built, so a trip by car took an entire day. In those days, certain people who owned cars would take passengers from city to city for a fee, and Uncle Jack had managed to find someone like this who would take me all the way to Cleveland. There were a few other passengers in the car who mostly dozed, but I was too excited to sleep. For one thing, I was riding in a brand-new car straight from the factory, something I'd never done before. For another, I couldn't believe how immense the country was, how many cities and houses and cars and farms and people were spread out over such a vast amount of land. I just had to get a good look at every single thing we passed along the way.

Once in Cleveland, I was dropped off at the home of my Aunt Helen (my mother's youngest sister) and her husband, my Uncle Bill. My Uncle Herman, who was a bachelor, also lived there, so right away I met one of the two uncles from Builder's Steel who used to send us packages. I didn't stay there long, however: within a couple of days, I was living in a nearby rooming house and was ready to start work at Builder's Structural Steel.

Builder's was housed in a large, three-story building on East 34th Street with a railroad track that ran straight into the building, so steel could be loaded and unloaded inside. I was surprised to see that a couple hundred people worked there, including those who actually handled, cut, packaged, and transferred the steel, as well as salesmen, accountants, secretaries, drivers, and managers. It was a pretty big operation.

The main office was on the top floor, while the shop, painting areas, and other areas were on the bottom floor. My first job was to carry orders from the office to other parts of the building. Back then, orders were always hand-written: "Cut the steel to such-and-such a size," "Paint this steel black and that steel yellow," "Drill holes in the beams," and so on. I took orders from the office and handed them to the people in the shop and then took lists of tasks that had been completed from the shop back to the office. I went up and down the stairs all day carrying orders and lists, and sometimes ran out to get sandwiches, hamburgers, or Cokes for various people. I had to go quite a long way to the market to pick up lunches and, since my English was not the best, got a lot of orders wrong. But this just made people laugh. One time I rattled off the lunch order to a guy at the deli, but got confused when he started asking me things like "You want salami?" I didn't know if he was asking if I wanted extra meat or extra sandwiches, so I just kept saying "Yeah, yeah." Then, when I brought the food to the men in the office upstairs at Builders, I had way too many sandwiches. One of them said good-naturedly, "Next time they'll sell you the whole store!"

"That's okay," I shot back. "I'll bring it over." Fortunately, everyone laughed and I didn't get in trouble for either my mistakes or my mouth.

After I'd been carrying orders and lists back and forth for a couple of months, Uncle Jack decided to put me under the wing of the plant superintendent, Clem Dobler, who taught me to paint beams and cut steel. And I slowly began to understand what my uncles did. Builder's was a steel warehouse and structural fabricator; it didn't actually produce steel, like U.S. Steel, Republic Steel, or the other mills. Instead, Builder's bought steel from the mills, usually excess prime steel from overruns, or "irregular" steel that wasn't perfect and couldn't be sold by the mill to its intended customers. Builder's would then break the excess prime steel into smaller packages that could be sold to customers who were too small for the mills to bother with. In many cases, Builder's would also cut the steel into different shapes, or paint it, drill holes in it, and so on, depending on what the customer requested. As for irregular steel, Builder's would figure out how to cut it into smaller pieces so that the good sections could be resold as prime steel in small lots, and the irregular sections could be used for other purposes. And sometimes Builder's would order steel from the mill on behalf of its customers.

While both Uncle Jack and Uncle Herman owned the business, Jack was the real boss, and he made all of the decisions. Herman, for the most part, just went along with whatever Jack wanted, as he only owned 10 percent of the business and didn't have a strong enough personality to take Jack on. Fortunately, Jack seemed to be doing a very good job.

As the head of Builder's, Uncle Jack was always in search of two things: steel that could be repackaged or fabricated, and customers who needed it. In that line of work, it wasn't just a matter of making a certain item and putting it into a store for customers to buy over and over again. You never knew exactly how much or what kind of steel you would have the next day, what form it would take, or what condition it might be in. You also didn't know who your customers would be or what they might need. This meant that Uncle Jack had to wheel and deal constantly. Meanwhile, steel prices were always going up and down, so even if he bought a piece of steel at what seemed to be a profitable price, if the prices suddenly dropped too far too fast, Builder's would be stuck. It was a difficult business. You had to be strong, take chances, and make the right decisions on the fly; those who weren't cut out for it would be out of business in no time. But it was also a gentleman's business, in which a handshake was all you needed to seal a deal.

The company's steel was used to make buildings and bridges and thousands of tons of reinforcing bars, which were used to build all of the highways in the area, as well as the bridges crossing the highways in Ohio and neighboring states. Some years later, in the early fifties, my uncles got the contract to supply steel for the rebuilding of Thistledown, the big racetrack just east of Cleveland. This was a very big deal. The racetrack's grandstand and clubhouse had burned down in 1944, but because of wartime restrictions on construction, it was nine long years before the racetrack reopened. My uncles' steel was an essential component of the $3 million rebuilding program.

I was so proud to be working at Builder's that I was willing to do any job and work overtime or on the weekends, even though I wasn't paid extra: family members didn't get overtime pay. I figured I'd been given a new life and a chance to succeed, so if the company wanted me to work overtime, I didn't mind.

I also wanted to know *everything* about the business, so I was forever asking questions like, "Why is this steel considered irregular?" "How come this steel is good for beams?" "Why do we use this kind of paint on that steel?" Any question I could think of, I asked. I also read all the orders and lists I delivered, trying to figure out how the business worked. I asked the salesmen why they wanted to sell this kind of steel to that customer, and so on. Uncle Jack saw that I was inquisitive and didn't seem to mind a bit. Maybe he even liked it, because he had some relatives on the payroll who were not so interested or inclined to work hard.

A good example of this was Samuel, the nephew of Jack's first wife, Ethel. It didn't matter what task they gave to Samuel, he did a lousy job. One time he was supposed to paint some steel beams and the connections that went with them (bolts and such) with a special paint made of red lead. He did paint the beams, although not all the way to their ends, but he didn't paint the connections. When I saw this, I asked him, "What are you doing? Why aren't you painting the whole thing?"

He just shrugged. "It doesn't matter."

"What do you mean it doesn't matter? You're supposed to do it right!"

He didn't care. I got angry because I knew that someone else would have to repaint it before we shipped it. He was wasting company money and hurting our reputation. So I went upstairs to tell Uncle Jack.

"Samuel isn't painting the beams properly," I told my uncle, before asking, "Why do you let him work here?"

Uncle Jack just smiled and shook his head. "Well, Morris, sometimes you do things for family," he replied. It didn't seem like a very good reason to me.

After that, I always called Samuel "Sam-mule" because I thought he was as dumb as a mule, and as stubborn as one, too. And Sam-mule must have complained about it to his aunt, because one day when I was in the car with Uncle Jack and Aunt Ethel, she turned and said to me, "Morris, why are you so mean to my relatives?"

"I'm not mean to them," I replied, stung. "What are you talking about?"

"Why do you call Samuel 'Sam-mule?'"

"Because he's dumb," I said. Uncle Jack roared with laughter and that was the end of that.

I always thought he liked me because I was inquisitive, and I always thought Aunt Ethel didn't like me because she had her own nephews and wanted them to be promoted. In the end, some of her nephews worked out all right, but others did not. I wasn't competing for Uncle Jack's favor by trying to make Samuel look bad. I just told him what I'd seen: that Samuel was hurting the company by doing a lousy job.

For me, it was always about doing a good job and making the company stronger, even under dangerous conditions. One frigid winter's day, I was almost killed unloading steel plates. The plates were 72" by 240" and were shipped from the mills in open gondolas (railway cars with four sides and no roof). The train carrying the steel plates ran straight into the plant on a special track that was depressed, so that the top edge of the gondola was at ground level, and anyone standing on the factory floor could easily climb right in.

I often unloaded these plates with my older brother Erwin, who had left Czechoslovakia shortly after me and was also working in the family business. The process went like this: We climbed into the gondola, which had enough space so we could walk around the stack of plates, and Erwin stood on one side while I stood opposite him. A crane above our heads dangled four chains that each had a special hook at its end. Erwin and I grabbed the chains and attached the hooks underneath the steel plate on the top of the stack, near its corners. When everything was hooked up properly, we gave the crane operator a signal and the crane lifted the plate out of the gondola, with the operator being very careful to keep everything level so the plate wouldn't slide. This was tedious work, and the crane operator needed to have a steady hand to keep the plate perfectly balanced. If all went well, the plates would eventually be stacked neatly on the factory floor.

On this particular winter day, it had rained the day before and we'd had a very cold night—below zero. My brother and I had just attached the hooks to a second plate and the crane began lifting it, when suddenly the plate lift began to slide! Because gondolas aren't covered, rain or snow can fall directly on the plates and turn into ice, which is exactly what had happened. This makes the plates very slippery and, in this case, the crane operator didn't keep the plate perfectly level. As soon as I saw that plate sliding toward me, I knew I had a few seconds to get out. I leapt out of the gondola and, a second later, the plate flew off the hooks and smashed against the gondola wall, right where I had been standing. If I'd been any slower, I'd have been a goner.

It may sound like my life was entirely about work, but that's really not the case. I was getting to know my new surroundings, little by little, and Uncle Herman helped me with that. While I admired Uncle Jack because he had built something from nothing, I actually felt closer to Uncle Herman because he spent time with me. As a bachelor with no children, he had plenty of spare time, and he would sometimes take me to dinner, to nightclubs and the like. We had a good time.

One time, we went to Solomon's Delicatessen, a very busy place with waiters who were, shall we say, less than polite. Uncle Herman ordered a tongue sandwich for me, and it was the first time I had ever had such a delicacy—it was delicious! But a few weeks later, when I went back to Solomon's by myself, I had trouble ordering the same thing. My English was still a little rough, so when the waiter, a big guy, came by and said curtly, "What do you want for lunch?" I blanked.

"Wait a minute," I said, flipping through my Slovak-English dictionary to find a translation of the Slovak word for "tongue" while the waiter stood there with an annoyed expression. Relieved that I found it fairly quickly, I looked up, smiled and announced proudly, "I want a language sandwich."

The waiter's face darkened with anger.

"You want a language sandwich, huh?" he said, grabbing me by the collar and lifting me out of my seat. "*I'll* give you a language sandwich!"

With that, he hustled me out the door and pushed me out onto the street. Yes, I was definitely getting acquainted with my new surroundings.

After I'd been working at Builder's for a while, Uncle Jack decided to take me with him to the other office, which was in Pittsburgh. This one did not have a plant attached; it was just an office where his employees bought and sold steel. Uncle Jack went there every so often to check on these men, and this time he took me along. On our way from Cleveland to Pittsburgh, I continually pointed out different mills and factories and asked my uncle what each one was, what was done there, and who owned them. Finally, he turned to me and asked, "Why do you want to know about every plant?

The answer was easy: "Because one day I'm going to own my own company. A big one."

Uncle Jack laughed delightedly.

Once we arrived in Pittsburgh, we drove to a nondescript building and climbed the stairs to a little room on the second story that served as his office. I remember being unimpressed as I stood leaning against a wall while Uncle Jack sat at his desk and looked over some papers. Sometime later, I was still standing there, idly watching people coming and going and trying to understand what they were saying, when a big, tough-looking fellow walked in and sat down opposite Uncle Jack. They began talking about some deal, and while I couldn't follow the conversation very well, I could tell that both men were getting angry. Suddenly the man reached into his coat pocket and pulled out a pistol! I don't know what he was planning to do with it, but Uncle Jack wasn't waiting to find out. Jack flew across the desk, grabbed the guy's hand, twisted it and smashed it against the desk until the gun clattered to the floor. Then my uncle grabbed the guy by the collar, lifted him to his feet, dragged him to the window and threw him straight through the glass! The window shattered and shards of glass flew everywhere as the guy tumbled two stories to the ground. An ambulance had to come and scrape him up off the sidewalk. Now *that* impressed me! I could see that my uncle was no one to fool with.

On the way back to Cleveland, I asked Uncle Jack what had happened, but he wouldn't say a word about it, so I never did find out why the guy had pulled a gun on him. And that wasn't the only time I saw Jack being tough. One time, he hired a company to put some columns up right outside of Builder's, and the company sent over a guy who began digging holes for the pillars. At some point,

Uncle Jack noticed that the guy was digging a hole right in front of a door where, obviously, we didn't want a column. The worker was standing in the hole, which was about three feet deep, when Uncle Jack went up to him and shouted, "You son of a bitch, I didn't tell you to put a pillar there!"

The guy just looked up, shrugged, and kept on digging. I could practically see the steam coming out of Uncle Jack's ears as he grabbed the guy by the collar, lifted him straight up out of the hole and set him roughly on the ground. Terrified, the guy grabbed his shovel, ran off, and never returned.

But Uncle Jack was always kind to me, and I got the feeling that I was, in a way, the son he never had. Sometimes he would ask me questions like, "What kind of steel do you think would be right for Mr. So-and-So?" or "Why should it be that steel and not some other kind?" It was as if he was testing me or trying to prepare me for a bigger and better position. If I didn't know the answer, he would say, "Go talk to someone and find out why." He knew that if I had to dig out the answer myself, it would make more of an impression than if he just told me the answer.

One thing I definitely wanted to find out about was driving. The company had a big freight truck that was parked right underneath our building. Since the building stood on pillars, there was enough room down there to house a truck. I had been watching the drivers pull that truck in and out of this parking area for weeks and really wanted to learn to drive it. I was so amazed by that truck and so interested in it that one of the drivers broke down and showed me how to start it, shift the gears, and step on the gas and the brake.

One day, when no one was around, I climbed into the cab, started up the truck, and put my foot on the gas pedal. The truck lurched forward a bit, which was exciting, but then it stopped. I couldn't figure out why, so gave it more gas. I kept giving it more and more gas when suddenly I realized that the whole building was shaking! This truck had some extensions on its sides to hold wide loads, and one of them had gotten caught on a pillar. I was making the truck engine work so hard and pulling so hard on that pillar, that the building was shaking under the strain. The shaking made just about everyone in the building run outside to see what was happening, and pretty soon they were all standing there laughing at me. I was so embarrassed, I almost cried.

But Uncle Jack wasn't laughing.

"Come upstairs!" he bellowed, and he then proceeded to bawl me out. Finally, when he was finished, he said to me in his sternest voice, "You want to learn how to drive?"

"Yeah," I replied, meekly.

"Well, we have people here who know how to drive. Go ask someone to teach you!"

I scurried out of his office realizing that, underneath it all, Uncle Jack was a pretty understanding guy.

You'd think that the incident with the truck would have been enough to keep me in line. But one day I decided I wanted to try operating the crane. I climbed up the ladder and got into the crane man's cab, which ran along heavy tracks that were attached to the walls. One of the operators had invited me into the cab once before and shown me how the levers operated, so I thought I could handle it.

Well, I couldn't. I did manage to maneuver the crane to the end of the tracks, where it hit the rubber bumper. That should have been a warning to me to stop, but I didn't understand what it meant, so I just kept giving it electrical power, trying to make the crane continue moving. I wound up blowing all the fuses and could have brought the whole thing crashing down, if certain people hadn't seen what I was doing and stopped me. Uncle Jack wasn't too happy about that little incident either. Not surprisingly, I got a bit of a reputation at Builder's for doing crazy things. It got to the point where Clem Dobler, the superintendent, would tell me to do something and then add, "Please, don't get me in trouble!"

After I had been working at Builder's for maybe two years, Uncle Jack called me in to his office and said simply, "Let's go to Niles." Niles was a suburb of Youngstown, Ohio, which was a big center for steel production. In the early part of the twentieth century, Youngstown and its surroundings were the second-largest steel-producing area in America, exceeded only by Pittsburgh. In and around Youngstown, there were hundreds of plants, warehouses, fabricators, and other businesses related to the steel industry. For miles along the Mahoning River, which runs through Youngstown and Niles and all the way into Pennsylvania, there was one steel mill after another. There were so many of these businesses, in fact, that sometimes it was hard to say where one ended and the next began. As we rode past steel mill after steel mill that day, I kept drifting off to sleep. I'd been out dancing the jitterbug and drinking the night before and wasn't in my finest form. The only reason I didn't sleep the entire way was my brother Erwin kept jabbing me in the ribs.

Once we arrived in Niles, Uncle Herman drove us to an unimpressive-looking factory called Allied Metals that was fairly close to downtown. There, Uncle Jack explained that he'd been doing business with Allied Metals for a long time. But because they owed him a lot of money that they couldn't repay, he had recently taken them over. And now he was in the process of putting his own people in place at Allied.

After we toured the plant, saw the offices, and walked around the outside of the buildings, Uncle Jack turned to me and asked, "Would you like to work here?"

I was taken aback for a minute. I really didn't want to leave Cleveland but was afraid to say so. Instead I said, "It's okay."

And that was that. A few days later I moved to Niles, rented a room, and began working at Allied Metals. I was the only member of my family there; there were no uncles, aunts, or cousins, and my brother stayed in Cleveland. I especially missed my young cousin Geri Polster, the daughter of Aunt Helen and Uncle Bill. About seven years younger than me, she was a delightful girl who brightened up any room just by walking in. I didn't see much of her after I moved to Niles, but I always remembered her standing outside her house in the snow, wearing a beautiful fur coat that Uncle Herman had bought for her, laughing and laughing. I don't remember what was so funny, just that she seemed to find joy in everything.

I felt completely alone in Niles. But I had a job to do, a new job at a new company.

Like Builder's, Allied bought steel from the mills, usually overruns of prime steel or irregulars. And, like Builder's, Allied would break the steel into smaller lots to sell to customers that were too small to deal with the mills. The difference was that while Builder's also processed the steel by cutting it, painting it, and drilling holes, Allied was a "stamper." It ran the steel through big stamping presses that pressed it into different shapes, like signs and auto parts. But even though Allied's machines and products were different from those at Builder's, the business was the same: find steel to buy from the mills, break it into smaller packages, often do some kind of work on it, and then sell it to customers all over the country. Both businesses were risky: buying too much steel that couldn't be sold quickly enough could result in a take-over or bankruptcy.

Uncle Jack wanted to make sure Allied did well, so he stole a very smart Welshman named Dudley Jones from one of our competitors and made him president of Allied. And, as expected, Dudley made lots of good deals and the company did well—or so I heard. I was so far down the ladder, I didn't even speak to the higher-ups. Dudley and the other executives would smile and wave if they saw me, but that was about it. Once in a while, Dudley, who was always a gentleman, would ask me how things were going.

When I started working at Allied, I performed many of same tasks that had been assigned to me at Builder's. But soon I was eager to do more, so I asked if I could learn to "mic" steel—that is, to use a device called a micrometer to gauge the thickness of a sheet of steel. This is very important, because you want the steel sheet to have an even thickness throughout. Prime steel is almost always perfect, the same thickness at both ends and at any point in the middle. But a sheet of irregular steel could be .0359 inches thick (20 gauge) in one area and .0489 inches (18 gauge) in another. We had to mic every sheet of irregular steel carefully so we knew exactly where to cut in order to produce pieces of an even gauge, and what each piece could be used for. I had to study the charts over and over again to figure out how to convert decimals into the gauges of different kinds of steel, and vice versa —which was especially tough for me since I was still accustomed to the metric system. I also learned how to inspect the steel for rust, bent edges, cracks, and other imperfections, and how to run the shear machine, which we used to make different sized cuts in the steel.

Before long, I began to love working at Allied, where I learned something new every day and was gradually given more and more responsibility. I was also making friends at the plant. The guys from the factory introduced me to some nice women, and we'd go bowling or get a pizza, but there was no one special. But since I was the only member of my family in Niles and didn't have a car, I couldn't just go back to Cleveland whenever I felt like it. Still, for the most part, everything was going well.

Then came December 7, 1941, when that dreadful announcement came over the radio telling us that the Japanese had bombed Pearl Harbor and destroyed the U.S. Naval Fleet. I didn't know anything about Pearl Harbor—not many people outside the Navy even knew where it was, because Hawaii wasn't a state yet. But that didn't matter. If America was going to war, I wanted to go, too.

CHAPTER FIVE

Love, War and Citizenship

On Monday morning, December 8, 1941, the day after what became known as Pearl Harbor Day, I went straight to my uncle's office and announced in no uncertain terms, "Uncle Jack, I want to join the Army and defend my country."

He looked at me for a long moment before saying flatly, "*Ear vait bakkomen gehergt,*" which is Yiddish for "You'll get killed."

"*Ich vait namen mine gycer,*" I shot back. *I'll take my chances.*

Uncle Herman, who had been sitting there reading a newspaper when I barged in, frowned at me and said, "What's the rush? Maybe the steel business will be declared essential and you won't have to go."

He didn't get it.

"I don't want a deferral," I said, annoyed. "I want to defend my country and get after the Nazis."

"Let's just wait a little and see what happens," Uncle Jack said soothingly. "Okay?"

But when pictures of our twisted, demolished ships were splashed across the pages of every single newspaper, when the body count of American sailors and soldiers rose beyond our worst expectations, and when the Japanese attacked American troops in the Philippines and the Pacific Islands without mercy, I became even more determined to go. Over the next couple of weeks, I marched up to Uncle Jack's office several times and declared my intentions, but his answer was always the same.

"Wait, wait," he would plead. "Just hold off for one more week."

"But I want to defend my country!"

"It's not *your* country," Uncle Herman would chime in. "You're still a greenhorn." That always made me furious.

"It *is* my country," I'd insist, even though I wasn't yet a citizen. "I'm an American!"

Although I wasn't truly an American citizen, I was halfway there. In those days, a person was granted U.S. citizenship in two stages. First you had to take an examination to see if you knew the most basic things about U.S. history and the ideas that formed the foundation of the government. This test had questions like, "Who was the first president of the United States?" and "Is a person considered innocent until he is proven guilty?" (I thought that being innocent until proven guilty was a wonderful idea. We didn't have that back in Czechoslovakia!) If you passed this test you got your first set of papers, but you had to wait a certain amount of time before taking a second test. I had passed the first test and was currently in the waiting stage. This meant I was not technically an American citizen, but I was on my way.

Still, Uncle Jack wasn't keen on my going to war. In spite of my protestations, he kept saying, "Let's wait one more week. We'll see what happens."

What happened was my number came up. I received my draft notice about six weeks after Pearl Harbor was bombed, in January 1942. (Yes, even if you weren't a citizen, if you were a resident, you had to register for the draft as soon as you were eligible.) And suddenly, like millions of other young American men, I was off to war. First stop: Fort Hayes in Columbus, Ohio, where I was inducted into the Army. We were physically examined, given written tests to see how smart we were and what we might be good at, sworn in, and handed our uniforms. In my heart of hearts, I really wanted to go into the Air Corps (which was part of the Army back then) so I could become a fighter pilot; that sounded very exciting. But I failed the test because I couldn't define the word "knoll," a word I'd never heard of before and have rarely heard since. Still, there was no arguing with the Army, so the Air Corps was not for me.

From Columbus, they sent me to basic training at Fort Custer, which was near Battle Creek, Michigan. During my two-month stay there, we arose at 4:00 every morning and spent the day marching, running, climbing ropes, and crawling along the ground. We trained with old World War I guns because there weren't enough modern guns to go around; the U.S. Army had been very small at the time Pearl Harbor was bombed, and it had to grow fast. Since it took a while to make enough new guns, uniforms, and other kinds of equipment, we all had to make do with what we had.

Of course, it wasn't all just marching and drilling. The bigwigs in the Army knew that soldiers need a little time off to have some fun, so every so often we were given passes to the USO (United Service Organization) in Battle Creek. The USO works to boost the morale of our military personnel. The idea, I suppose, is that the soldiers are performing a big service for the civilians, so the civilians want to do something nice for the soldiers in return. In Battle Creek, as in most cities, that "something nice" often took the form of dances full of pretty local girls who were happy to dance with soldiers and sailors far from home.

Like most other soldiers, I was more than eager to go to these dances, if only to be around some nice-looking women. So one weekend when I was off duty, I wandered over to the USO, which was hosting a dance with a live band. I loved to jitterbug and could do the fox trot and a few other dances, so I knew I was in for a good time. I walked into the big multipurpose room where the dance was being held, looked around, saw a nice-looking girl, and immediately asked her to dance. I definitely wasn't shy!

From then on, I danced every dance with one girl after another. That is, until my eye was drawn to a gorgeous brunette whose graceful moves on the dance floor set her apart from everyone else. Even though I was dancing with another girl at the time, I just couldn't stop staring at that stunning brunette. She had to be the most beautiful girl I had ever seen. Up until that moment, I hadn't been the least bit shy about walking up to a girl to ask her to dance. But with this one, I didn't want to take the chance of getting shut down. So instead, I went up to another girl, a pretty blonde, who was talking with a group of guys and seemed to be outgoing. I could sense that she would be easy to talk to.

After exchanging a few pleasantries, I indicated the brunette with a nod and said to the blonde, whose name was Joanne, "Say, who's that young lady over there?"

"Oh, that's my sister," she said off-handedly, surprising the hell out of me.

"Your *sister*?! Boy, you don't look anything alike!"

She laughed. "I know. Do you want to meet her?"

Did I? You bet I did! She took my hand and led me over to her sister, who turned and met my gaze with her beautiful dark brown eyes.

"Phyllis, meet Morris," Joanne said simply. Phyllis smiled at me, and right then and there I fell for her, big time.

It was all I could do to say, "Would you care to dance?"

Suddenly we were out on the floor and she was in my arms, which was exactly where I wanted to keep her for the rest of the evening. We danced every single dance after that, and once we started talking, we just couldn't stop. She told me about Chicago, where she lived with her family and was going to a business college while working in an attorney's office. And she told me about Battle Creek, where she and her sister were currently visiting relatives. I told her about Cleveland and my job at Builder's. And I even told her that I didn't know what had become of my parents and younger brothers back in Czechoslovakia. No one had heard a word from them, although there was still a chance that they might survive the war. It wasn't something I talked about often, but there was something about Phyllis that made me want to tell her everything.

We talked and danced for what seemed like forever that night. And by the end of the evening, I told Phyllis with absolute certainty, "I'm going to marry you." She just laughed. It must have seemed ridiculous to her. After all, she was going back to Chicago the very next day.

At some point during the evening, Joanne gave me a slip of paper with their Chicago address, but once I got back to the base, I realized I had lost it. Panicked, I went back to the USO the next time I was able to leave the base and told the girl behind the desk that I had lost the address of a very special girl. She was sympathetic but firm when she said that she was not allowed to give out the addresses of the USO girls.

I *did* know that the two sisters had been staying with their aunt, who came from a family by the name of Weiss that owned a dry cleaning business. It didn't take long before I found myself talking to a woman at Weiss's Cleaners, explaining that I was looking for two sisters from Chicago. I told her that I wanted to write a letter to one of the sisters to thank her for being so nice to me at the dance. What I didn't know was that the family already knew that Phyllis had met a young man from Europe at the dance. Otherwise, that nice woman probably wouldn't have given me her address. But she did, and to me it was like pure gold: 1478 Gregory Street, Chicago, Illinois.

Once I got that address, I wrote Phyllis a letter—with the help of my trusty Slovak-English dictionary, of course. After slaving over the letter and rewriting it a few times, I finally slid it into an envelope, addressed it, and dropped it in the mail. There was just one small problem: I had forgotten that her name was Phyllis: somehow, in my mind, her name was Sophie. I found out later that when Phyllis received my letter, she laughed out loud. And the next time she saw me, she couldn't resist saying, "You're going to marry me, but you can't even remember my name?"

Once I had finished my training at Fort Custer, I was sent on to Fort Sill, Oklahoma, where we learned how to fire artillery. The most important part of the whole process was properly calculating the trajectory of the artillery shell, so you would know how to angle the gun. The sergeant would tell us to hit a target that was, say, 2,000 yards away. Then, in a very short period of time, we had to go through the calculations, move the gun barrel up or down, right or left, and fire, fingers crossed. We were allowed three shots, two of which were supposed to help us "find the target." The first shot might fall a little short, the second might go a bit too far, but the third was supposed to be dead on. Those who couldn't manage to do this were out. Luckily, I was pretty good at hitting the target. It might have been because I had worked with numbers to mic the steel or because I had good depth perception. Whatever the reason, I could usually hit the target on the second shot.

My third stop was Camp Hood, Texas, a brand new base where we soldiers were trained to operate tank destroyers. I'm not talking about tanks, I'm talking about *tank destroyers*, which were big armored half-tracks, each outfitted with a large cannon and machine guns. Tank destroyers were created because our American tanks, which were called Sherman tanks (after Civil War hero General William Tecumseh Sherman), weren't as big or as mighty as the German tanks, which had thicker armor and more powerful cannon. If a Sherman went one-on-one against a German tank, it would probably lose. So we came up with tank destroyers to eliminate the enemy tanks before they got close enough to destroy our tanks. The tank destroyers were not designed to engage German tanks in direct combat. Instead, they were supposed to hang back and fire at the enemy tank's weakest points, the treads or the bottom of the turret. The unit patch we wore on our shoulders perfectly illustrated what we were supposed to do: It showed a tiger face with a German tank in its jaws, snapping the tank in two.

I learned a lot of things at Camp Hood: how to drive a tank destroyer, how to fire the main cannon, and how to fire and repair the machine guns, as well as how to use pistols and bazookas. I soon became a machine gun expert. In class, our instructor used to take a machine gun apart, mix up the pieces, and then tell us to reassemble the weapon. I was always the first to finish.

By this point, like many other soldiers, I was more than eager to get into battle. But I still had more training to do before I could go to Europe and take on the Nazis. After Camp Hood, they sent me to Fort Lewis in Washington state, where we practiced aiming at and shooting cannons at targets, over and over again.

One day my captain called me into his office. "Friedman," he said, "One of these days, this company is going to go overseas and fight. But since you're not a citizen, you don't have to go. If you want, you can stay here when we ship out, and they'll transfer you to some other unit that stays stateside."

This was the last thing I wanted to hear. Stay in the States after all of this training? No way.

"No, I want to go to Europe, sir," I insisted. "What do I need to do to go?"

"Are you *volunteering* to go?"

"Yes. I want to go."

"Okay, then. You're going." It was as simple as that.

Once I had officially volunteered to go to war, the Army arranged for me to take my second citizenship test right away. I went to one of the courthouse buildings in Olympia, took the second exam, and passed with flying colors. And at long last, I was a citizen—an American!

Not long after that, we got our orders to ship out. Everyone in my unit was given one last furlough so we could see our families before going off to war. Naturally, I used mine to go to Chicago to see Phyllis. I flew there on a civilian plane and it was wonderful to see her. Unfortunately, I had to cut my visit short to go to Cleveland to see Uncle Jack and the rest of the family. But I would have much rather spent the entire time with Phyllis!

Then, in what seemed like the blink of an eye, my unit was on a train bound for New Jersey, then taken to New York Harbor, where we boarded the massive ocean liner, the *Queen Elizabeth*, for our voyage to England. It was April 19, 1944, and as the ship slowly pulled out of the harbor, I stood on the deck amid a crowd of other soldiers and watched the Statue of Liberty growing smaller and smaller, until finally it disappeared. It was a profound moment for me. The sight of that statue had signaled the beginning of a completely new life for me when I arrived back in 1936. Eight years later, as I watched it recede, I was on my way to an uncertain future. I knew very well that this could be the last time I ever saw Lady Liberty.

My unit ended up in Stratford-on-Avon, Shakespeare's birthplace, in the southern Warwickshire district of England. I knew nothing about Shakespeare back then and, of course, we had no time for the Royal Shakespeare Theatre or Anne Hathaway's cottage. Instead, we trained morning, noon, and night with the tank destroyers. Every morning we got up, marched, and worked on our rifle skills, shooting round after round at targets, learning to get the enemy before they got us. We also practiced driving a half-track (combination tank and truck) that had a new cannon that fired 3-inch shells powerful enough to disable a tank. We learned to situate the cannon on slopes, using the natural contours of the land to our advantage, and to set up camouflage. I also took a six-week course in the identification of enemy and allied aircraft, which taught me to distinguish between our planes and those of the enemy.

We arrived in England during the spring of 1944, when (as everyone knew) the American and British armies were getting ready for a big invasion of Europe. We didn't know where or when this would occur, but we knew it was coming. That invasion, which came to be known as D-day, finally took place on June 6 on the cold, windswept beaches of Normandy, France. Five days later, our unit landed on that same beach and waded ashore. We had been held back for five days because a massive amount of infantry had been sent in to seize the beaches and start the move inland. By the time we arrived, some 325,000 troops, 55,000 vehicles, and 100,000 tons of supplies had already landed on the beaches. With all that infantry safely ashore, they now needed tank destroyers, and that was what we had to offer. Nobody was shooting at us, thank God, as we trudged down the ramp of the landing craft and waded ashore through those frigid waters, hoisting our rifles over our heads so they wouldn't get wet. But we could see the remains of the bloody battles that had occurred there just days earlier. Blasted tanks, trucks, and jeeps had been pushed aside in big heaps, and there were bodies still bobbing in the water. We marched across the beach and then up into the hills, stopping a little way behind the frontlines to begin digging our foxholes.

I was with the Headquarters Company, 4th Tank Destroyers. You might think that we just handled training, supplies, and paperwork, but we actually saw a lot of action. We shot up German tanks, and sometimes a few of us would be picked to scout the local terrain. This happened to a good friend of mine from Cleveland named McDermott. I hadn't known him in Cleveland; we met in the Army. But we became friends and shot craps, played pool and poker, and hung out together. He was a tall, slim young man who was very funny and always smiling. I liked him a lot. We often talked about him coming to visit me in Niles after the war was over.

One night, the sergeant pointed to McDermott and another guy, who I didn't know well, and said, "You and you. Grab your rifles and go scouting."

"Scouting" meant sneaking up to the enemy lines and, if you could, getting behind them. Once you'd gotten as close as you could, you were supposed to estimate the number of men and tanks the enemy had, figure out where they were dug in, and so on. All of this would be very valuable information for your unit *if* you managed to make it back safely.

So McDermott and the other guy sneaked off into the darkness to do their duty. They never returned. Someone told me that they found my friend dead, his head blown off by a potato masher (the German version of a grenade). And I heard that the other soldier had been badly wounded in the back but was rescued and shipped home. But that's how things went during wartime: one minute your best friend was standing next to you smoking a cigarette and telling you a dirty joke; the next minute he was gone forever. You couldn't allow yourself to worry that it might be *you* some day, or someone you knew and cared about. If you thought about it at all, the unlucky person always had to be some nameless, faceless stranger.

By July, we had advanced inland to the little French village of Saint-Lô, where the Germans were firmly planted and determined to keep us at bay. They knew that if we broke through their lines, they would be finished. As for us, we constantly lived on the edge: slightly behind the front lines, we were always ready to jump into our foxholes and take cover. Shells flew back and forth overhead.

One time, after we dove into our foxholes, a shell landed so close to me that the explosive force smacked both sides of my head like a ton of bricks. Blood started coming out of my ears, and I was so confused I crawled out of my foxhole and started running. I have no idea where I thought I was going, but thank God my sergeant grabbed me and threw me into a foxhole, probably saving my life.

Although theoretically I handled paperwork, supplies, and training, in battle conditions I did whatever I was told. Every morning the sergeant looked at his list and said, "Friedman, today you will ..." And whatever he said, I did, whether it was checking trucks and half-tracks, stripping and cleaning machine guns, or whatever else he wanted.

Then finally, in late July, we broke out of the Normandy beachhead and fanned out across northern France. General Omar Bradley launched a massive attack on the Germans called Operation Cobra. The little village of Saint-Lô was targeted by three thousand airplanes that bombed and shot the hell out of the Germans encamped there. Then, American troops and tanks swarmed in, and after a few days of hard fighting, the Germans were on the run. From that point on, we were moving fast.

My company raced ahead with the rest, shooting up German tanks that hadn't retreated fast enough. The German lines started crumbling as they scrambled to get out of France and back to Germany, and our guys were right on their tails, pounding them every step of the way. As for my headquarters unit, because the frontlines were moving so quickly, we began to lag farther behind the lines. But we weren't exactly out of danger. Once, as I was standing outside with a group of guys, a shell exploded some distance away and sent shrapnel zinging through my pants. It never touched my leg, but it was a little too close for comfort.

When the lines stabilized near the French-German border in the late fall of 1944, things slowed down for us. My unit set up headquarters in a chateau not too far from Fontainebleau, the fancy royal "hunting lodge" south of Paris. Since we were safely behind the lines, I was feeling cocky enough one afternoon to go off for a walk by myself. I ended up in a nearby village, where I struck up a conversation with a farmer named Deux. He knew a little English, I knew a little French, we used a lot of sign language, and we became friends right away. After that, I went to his house for dinner almost every night and brought the Deux family food that I had "liberated" from the officers' mess.

As the supply officer, I was in charge of supplying the officers' mess hall. So, in order to get food for the Deux family, I'd assign a big can of peaches, for example, to the officers' mess, "forget" to give them the can, and then take it with me. If someone asked me about the can of peaches, I would say it had been assigned to the officers. If they pressed me about what happened to it, I'd just say, "I don't know. Ask the officers." Naturally, nobody wanted to do that. The Deux family had a very pretty daughter, and I would have liked to have gotten closer to her, but they were strict Catholics and, as we used to say, "She would go so far, but no farther."

My good times with the Deux family came to an abrupt end on December 16, 1944, when huge German tank forces crashed through the Ardennes forest, catching us by surprise and smashing through our lines in the early days of what became known as The Battle of the Bulge. Our generals were very worried: the Germans were pounding us, scattering our troops and causing tremendous amounts of damage. We needed as many men with rifles as possible on the front lines, but it would take too long to ship them over from Britain or America. So the generals ordered everyone into battle: cooks, clerks, supply officers, and everyone else behind the lines was given a rifle and sent to the front. I was no exception: after being handed a rifle, I was put on a truck bound for who knows where. It looked like I was finally going to the front.

Instead, I wound up working at a prisoner-of-war camp. Several hundred Germans, Hungarians, and other enemy soldiers flooded in every day, and we herded them inside a big compound surrounded by a wire fence. Then we stood guard outside to make sure they didn't escape. Sometimes, when a fight broke out between the prisoners, one of us had to go inside the wire fence carrying only a baton, while another guard watched from the outside. We had been warned that taking a sidearm inside the compound was too dangerous; someone might take it away and use it against you. So when we went in to break up a fight, all we had was a baton. Once inside the compound, we knew better than to let the prisoners surround us, and our fellow guards outside the compound always kept a close eye on us.

While I was guarding the prisoners, American and British forces not only stopped the German advance but also began to push them back. The Battle of the Bulge turned out to be a very bad idea for the Germans. They lost precious men, tanks, and supplies, but got nothing in return. And once the battle was over, we swept into Germany, demolishing the remnants of their crumbling army as we went. Meanwhile, the Russians poured into Germany from the east, killing even more German soldiers and destroying even more of their tanks and weapons. The Germans were hammered by the Americans and British from the west and the Russians from the east. And by early May, the war was over—at least, the war in Europe.

The Army gave its soldiers points for time served, participating in battle, being married, and other things. The points were then used to determine who was eligible for discharge and when. At the time that Germany surrendered, I was a few points shy of the number I needed to go home: I had eighty-two or eighty-three points, while eighty-five was the golden number. So even though the war in Europe was over, I was still in the Army and slated to be shipped to the Pacific to fight Japan. But before I got any orders, my captain called me in. He indicated a stack of papers in his hand and said, "You're from Czechoslovakia, aren't you?"

"Yes, sir!"

"And you speak Slovakian, right?"

"Yes, sir!"

"Well, soldier, we can use you here. We need someone to interrogate prisoners, translate documents, and things like that. You can go through some training, become a warrant officer, and stay here in Europe."

This made plenty of sense and was a whole lot safer than being shipped halfway around the world to invade Japan, where my chances of getting killed were high. People were saying we would lose half a million men, maybe a million, in the invasion of Japan—a lot more than we had lost in the fight against Germany.

But I didn't even have to think twice about my answer. I knew what I wanted.

"I would prefer to go home on furlough, and then go on to Japan, sir."

What I *really* wanted to do was go home and see Phyllis. And if that meant I'd end up taking a trip to Japan, so be it. By that time, we had been corresponding for three years, and all I wanted was to be with her. The entire time I'd been gone, I'd dreamed about beating the Germans so I could go home and be with Phyllis. I must admit this feeling was intensified by letters she'd written me about visiting wounded soldiers in the hospital in Battle Creek. I sure didn't want her getting too close to any of them, not with me so far away!

That's how I came to be back in the States on leave by the end of July 1945. Naturally, I made a beeline for Phyllis in Battle Creek, which upset my family in Cleveland. But I didn't care. I told Phyllis right away that I wanted to marry her then and there, but her father put his foot down.

"You'll have to wait until the war is over in Japan before you can marry my daughter," he said firmly.

"Okay," I said, knowing I wasn't going to change his mind.

Naturally I was upset that I couldn't marry Phyllis right away, but I really did understand. Her father wasn't sure that I'd come home in one piece—or come home at all. The Japanese had fought like hell all through the war, and they were more than willing to kill themselves with their kamikaze airplanes and banzai charges, as long as they took as many Americans with them as possible. Everyone knew that the invasion of Japan was going to be bloody. But I also knew, deep in my soul, that I'd be back.

And then Divine Providence intervened. In August, the U.S. dropped two atomic bombs on Japan, and the war was over, once and for all. I was at a base in Indiana when it happened, and right away I told my officer that I was about to get married, so it was important for me to get out of the Army as soon as possible. I thought he was going to tell me to take a hike, but he didn't. And in no time, I was out.

As soon as they handed me my papers, I rushed into town, bought a civilian suit, and hopped on a train to Battle Creek, where Phyllis and her family were living. I thought I would surprise them, but Phyllis had called the base looking for me and found out I had left. She then looked at the train schedules, figured out when I was going to arrive, and got her whole family to come to her house and welcome me home. They were all waiting for me with hugs and big smiles when I walked up and rang the doorbell. It was one of the happiest days of my life.

CHAPTER SIX

Quit *Hocking* Me Already!

World War II was finally over. I was twenty-five years old, had survived the war in one piece, and had only one thing on my mind: I wanted to marry Phyllis. Fortunately, she was for it, and so were her parents. In fact, right away her father said, "We'll make you a nice wedding right here in Battle Creek."

That sounded great to us. But when I called my own family to tell them I was getting married, Uncle Herman was less than pleased.

"Battle Creek?" he roared. "Why do you want to get married there? Come to Cleveland and *we'll* make you a wedding. A big wedding, with a band and a singer. It will be a real party!"

Phyllis and I liked that idea even better, so we took her mother, Rose, with us to Cleveland to start making arrangements. But from the moment we arrived, Uncle Herman started throwing up roadblocks. For starters, he had an annoying habit of taking me aside and asking me some very direct questions about Phyllis.

"She doesn't *look* Jewish," he whispered to me, early on. "Are you sure she's Jewish?"

"Of course she's Jewish. She's Jewish, her mother is Jewish, her mother's mother is Jewish; they're *all* Jewish!"

But Uncle Herman was unconvinced.

"She's doesn't look it. How can she be Jewish when her skin is so dark?"

He was really starting to get under my skin. "*Hock mir nicht kein chinik,*" I snapped at him, which in Yiddish means "Don't bang my tea kettle," or more to the point, "Stop driving me crazy!"

It soon became clear that Uncle Herman and most of the rest of the family did not approve of Phyllis and were dead set against the wedding, in spite of his earlier offer to "make a real party." I don't know how anyone could be against Phyllis, who was the sweetest, most beautiful girl in the world. Any man would be proud to have her as his wife. But they thought Phyllis was too American and too modern—after all, she wore an ankle bracelet! She was nothing like the traditional, Old Country kind of girl they had in mind for me. Phyllis was too refined and too educated to be a good wife, in their view. And she was a *Reform* Jew, which, as far as they were concerned, meant she really wasn't Jewish at all. I guess I shouldn't have been too surprised to find that Uncle Herman wasn't making any plans to rent a hall or hire a caterer or anything else, despite his promises.

To make matters worse, it wasn't only me he was *hocking* (driving crazy). He was also saying crazy, rude things to both Phyllis and her mother and in general trying to break us up. He would say things to Phyllis like "What do you want to marry *him* for?" And he would ask her mother things like, "What are you, *schnorrers,* thinking you can get us to pay for the wedding?" *Schnorrer* is a Yiddish word that means "beggar."

After a few days of insults and incredible rudeness, Rose got fed up and said to Phyllis, "Let's go home. You don't want to get mixed up with this family."

When I heard this, I took Phyllis aside in a panic and said, "Listen, you're not marrying my family, you're marrying me. And I love you and will always work hard for you. Let's forget my family, go to New York, and get married on our own."

And that's exactly what we did. We put Rose on a train back to Battle Creek, then got on a different train bound for New York City. I was hurt and embarrassed by the way my family had treated us and didn't give a damn if I ever saw any of them again.

Once we got to New York, we rushed around and got the blood tests and the necessary papers and finally got married in a little rented hall. We actually did have a few family members present, including my Uncle Harry and Aunt Rose from the Bronx, who had taken me in when I first arrived in this county and treated me like one of their own. Their daughter, my beautiful cousin Gertrude, was also there, and during the days before the wedding, she had fun being Phyllis's chaperone. (Back then, an unmarried young woman could not spend time with a man unless she was chaperoned.) There was also my father's brother Jack—not Uncle Jack from Cleveland, who was my mother's brother. This Uncle Jack had come to America from Czechoslovakia years earlier when his family wanted to hire a matchmaker to find him a wife.

After the wedding, Phyllis and I went to a resort in the Catskills for our honeymoon, then took the train back to Cleveland to face my family as a married couple. I had sent them all telegrams announcing the wedding, but I hadn't heard anything from anyone. Once we arrived, the reception my family offered was not cordial. Even my own sister, who was now living in Cleveland, was not very welcoming. When I went to visit her, she came outside to talk with us but never invited us in. Luckily, my brother-in-law Henry invited us in. When we went to Uncle Jack's house and knocked on the door, his wife Ethel invited us in. But while Aunt Ethel was hospitable, Uncle Jack was simply polite. He said "hello" and "best of luck to you," but that was it, and we left after maybe four or five minutes. To hell with them, I thought.

From Cleveland, Phyllis and I traveled to Battle Creek, where the reception was about as different as night and day. Everyone was so happy to see us, and Phyllis's parents invited us to move into a bedroom on the top floor of their house. We hauled our luggage up the stairs, opened the door to the bedroom, and found a beautiful bouquet of roses waiting for us on the nightstand. Right next to it was a check for three thousand dollars.

"This is what we would have spent on the wedding," Phyllis's father, George, told us. "Since you eloped, you can take the money. It will give you a start."

Three thousand dollars is a decent amount of money today, but back then it was a fortune. If you earned fifty dollars a week you were doing all right, meaning three thousand was enough to last more than a year.

So there I was, fresh out of the Army, married to the most wonderful woman in the world, and living in Battle Creek, Michigan. Of course, I had no job, since I no longer lived anywhere near the family businesses in Cleveland and Niles. But I had plenty of money in the bank, so I didn't bother to look for work for a while. Instead, Phyllis and I spent our time having fun and being in love.

Naturally, I knew the money wasn't going to hold out forever and I would have to find a job sooner or later. I probably could have worked for Phyllis's father, who was a painting contractor with maybe a dozen people working for him. But he made only a modest living, and I wanted a bigger life than that. Even though I felt like I belonged with her family, I didn't see a big enough future for us in Battle Creek. I'd seen what money could buy: the enormous steel mills and auxiliary businesses in Cleveland and Niles; Uncle Jack's beautiful house; the brand-new cars driven by steel company executives; expensive, top-quality clothing. Those were the things that I wanted.

So while we were still living in Battle Creek, we took the train to Youngstown, because that was the home of steel businesses, and that's what I knew. I wasn't looking for a specific job, but I did go to see Dudley Jones at Allied.

One of the first things he said was, "Are you coming back?"

"I don't know," I answered, shaking my head. I really didn't.

A few days later, I happened to walk past the Youngstown Club, which was downtown and had a fancy restaurant on the second story. It was a "restricted place," meaning no Jews allowed, but I knew my Uncle Jack had gone there as a guest of Dudley Jones, who was not Jewish.

Just as I was walking by, Uncle Jack's lawyer, Mr. Freelander, walked out the club's front door. His face lit up when he saw me and he smiled broadly. "Morrie," he shouted. "How you doing? Come on over here." He waved me over toward the entrance to the club and shook my hand.

"You've got a wife now," he said, patting me on the shoulder approvingly. "You gotta go to work. So where you going to work?" I knew he was not just asking me because he was curious; he was asking for my uncle, who was wondering what the hell I was up to. I thought maybe Uncle Jack was sitting up in the restaurant, had seen me coming through the window, and had sent his attorney down to talk to me.

"Tell my uncle I'll go to work when I'm ready," I replied. Then I patted his shoulder, smiled, and went on my way.

A few weeks later, I left Phyllis back in Battle Creek and took a quick trip to Niles, where I rented a room and went to see Dudley. I was ready to return to work.

One of the first things he asked me was, "Did you talk to your uncle?" He wanted to know if any arrangements had been made for my return to work.

"No. Since I'll be working for you, I came to see you first."

Dudley liked that and said he looked forward to my returning to Allied.

Then I finally bit the bullet and drove to Builder's in Cleveland to see Uncle Jack. He gave me just a minute or two of his time, but just like that I was back working at Allied. Uncle Herman was very friendly, especially the first time he saw me back at work. He put his arm around my shoulders and told me how happy he was to see me.

I picked up where I had left off, working part-time in the shipping office and part-time in the plant, where I mic'd the steel and did anything I was asked to do. Right away I saw that the business was different. During the war, the economy had revved up because we needed to produce things for the military. Military needs were given top priority, so most of the steel that was produced in those days was used to make jeeps, tanks, ships, weapons, Quonset huts, and the like. At that time, it was practically impossible for regular people to buy, say, a new car or a refrigerator. Nobody was making such things.

Then, once the war was over, the economy really boomed because the soldiers came home, married their girls, and suddenly needed houses, cars, refrigerators, radios, and a million other things. People began to have money in their pockets and were itching to buy everything they had been deprived of during four long wartime years, and the Great Depression before that. This is when I came back to the business—a time when factories were using so much steel that it started getting scarce. It was very difficult to get steel from the mills unless you were one of their very big customers. This was a big problem for Allied and Builder's, businesses that were based on buying prime overruns and irregular steel for resale. If we couldn't get steel, we were finished. The up-side of the scarcity was that when we *did* get steel, it was very easy to resell. Companies located throughout the country called us constantly to ask us to use our connections with the mills to get steel for them.

Fortunately, there *was* a way that we could get our hands on a great deal of steel: we could buy it straight from the government. Once the war ended, the government suddenly found itself in possession of all kinds of surplus materials, including tons and tons of steel. And it was willing to sell tons at modest prices, to anybody. Veterans, however, had first dibs, as a sort of "thank you" for the years they had spent fighting for our country. Because of this, I suddenly became a valuable commodity to Allied.

I hadn't been back on the job for long when I got a call from Uncle Jack, who told me that Dudley was going to talk to me about using my veteran status to buy surplus steel for Allied. Sure enough, Dudley called me into his office and asked me to fill out a form certifying I was a veteran and was buying steel for my own profit. That last part was very important: a veteran could buy the steel on behalf of a company, and the company could put up the purchase money, but that veteran *had* to profit from the sale. Dudley explained that he was going to use my veteran's status to bid on some surplus steel. He told me how much steel we were going to buy, and who he planned to sell it to. But a portion of this steel would be stored in the warehouse at Allied, and that was *my* steel, the part I had to sell to make the deal with the government legal. True to his word, Dudley had the steel deposited in the warehouse, where it sat while I called around to various customers, asking if they'd like to buy it. I soon sold it to Lou Tripodi at Niles Machine and Welding—my first sale!

A lot of the steel we purchased from the government was kept in a depot in Milwaukee, and from there we shipped it either to Allied or directly to the customers. Keeping our steel in that government depot created a big problem for us. There was so much steel going in and out of that place that it could take forever for them to load our steel on the train cars and ship it. We sometimes waited for months. And they never told us when they planned to ship it; it just arrived. In June of 1946, Dudley sent me to see if I could speed things up a little, so I made an appointment with the supervisor of the depot's yard and visited him in Milwaukee. We talked a bit, then I took him to dinner and explained that we needed to get our steel right away because if the market suddenly dropped, we would lose money.

"Okay," he said, agreeably. "I'll give you six cars right away."

This was great! Getting six railroad cars right away meant we could ship a lot of our steel. But even though we had six cars assigned to our steel, the guys working the yard weren't very good at loading and didn't put forth much effort. I noticed that at any given time, half the guys would be loading while the other half were drinking coffee. Then they would switch. I got them to load the cars a lot more quickly by bringing them food.

During my trip to Milwaukee, I stayed in Chicago at the LaSalle Hotel, a very nice, twenty-two-story hotel on the west side frequented by many very famous people. I couldn't believe how lucky I was to be staying on the sixteenth floor in such a nice place, until the night of June 5, when the entire hotel caught fire. It started on the first floor and spread quickly, trapping a lot of people on the higher floors—including me. Luckily, I was in pretty good shape, having been out of the Army less than a year. I was awakened by the sound of explosions and smelled smoke, so I hurried out into the hallway to see if I could walk down the stairs. Unfortunately, they were blocked. And as I turned back and was heading to the end of the hallway, I saw a young man who wasn't looking so good—he seemed sick and his skin had a grayish look. I thought he might have inhaled a lot of smoke. I put my arm around him, under his arms, and helped him down the hallway, where we were able to go through an open window to the fire escape and climb down the ladder all the way to the ground. Once we got out into the fresh night air, he recovered quickly and told me he had been in the Marines during the war. I was very surprised to read a story about the fire in the local paper the next day that mentioned an ex-solider saving an ex-marine. According to them, I was some kind of hero! I guess they must have interviewed him, because I certainly didn't say anything about it. But there were a lot of people who helped other people that night. It had nothing to do with heroism; it's just what you did during difficult times. Unfortunately, not everyone was as lucky as the Marine and I had been. A lot of people died, and City Hall had to be turned into a makeshift morgue to handle all the bodies. There had been a lot of near misses in my life: escaping Europe in time, almost being crushed by the sliding steel plate, surviving the shelling and shrapnel in World War II, and now this. I felt blessed.

Back at work, I was itching to learn more and do more and began to ask Dudley to give me extra tasks. I never asked for a promotion or to become his assistant; I simply said, "What else can I do for you?" Dudley was in his fifties by then, which seemed pretty old to me at the time, and he liked to take long client lunches that involved a few drinks and lots of schmoozing. It's not surprising, then, that he wasn't too energetic in the afternoons. That's when I usually did things for him, like talking to the shop superintendent about machinery, or tracking down a missing supply order. And slowly but surely, Dudley began to let me do more and more of his work.

He also taught me things directly, like how to sell steel, which is not as simple as it sounds. "You don't just call up a company and say, 'Do you want to buy two tons of 14 gauge prime?'" he told me. "A sale is conducted more like a dance."

It wasn't long before I learned to do that dance. It works like this: Let's say you just acquired some 14 gauge prime steel sheets from an overrun at a steel mill and it's sitting on your warehouse floor. If you knew that Company X was looking for exactly that, you would call the person in charge of buying and say, "I might have some 14 gauge sheets, but I don't know the quality or the length. And I don't know what size, gauge, and length you need." Of course, you actually *do* know what he needs because you've already quietly asked around. But you don't say so.

Then maybe he tells you something about what his company needs. Let's say he needs some prime steel that's cut to a certain length. You say, "Okay. Let me see what I can do."

A few days later, you call back and say, "Hey, I might be able to get some tons for you, cut to your size." You are careful to say you "might be able to get," even though you have exactly that sitting in your warehouse.

He might reply, "Well, we really need six tons. Can you get that?"

You answer, "I'll see what I can do. Call me back tomorrow."

When he calls you the next day, you tell him, "Well, it was difficult, but I got it for you. I can give you three tons at five cents a pound, and the other three tons at six cents a pound." Charging two different prices for the same steel may sound a little crazy, because you've paid the same price for all of it. But charging the two prices makes it seem as if you had to go to two different mills to get this steel for him, so fulfilling his order took a lot more effort than it actually did. This is important, because if you just call someone and say, "I have six tons of 14 gauge prime sheet in my warehouse right now," they will know you're eager to sell it. In fact, they will know that you *have* to sell it, because you sank money into the purchase and now you have to move it to get your money back, plus a little profit so you can buy some more steel. They will feel like they have you over a barrel and haggle with you over the price.

I loved learning things like this, as well as dealing with suppliers and helping to run the plant. I learned more about the business every day, as I took on more of Dudley's tasks. But there was one thing Dudley would never do: he would never take me with him on his visits to the steel mills. This was a big limitation for me, because everything started with the mills. Companies like ours that sold overruns and irregulars and small orders were entirely dependent on the good will of those in power at the steel mills. Naturally, they were going to sell loads of prime steel to their big customers like Ford and General Motors, whether they liked these customers or not. But for small customers like us, it was only because of good relations with the mills that we got any steel at all. If you wanted to run a company like Allied or Builder's, you had to have personal contact with certain people at the mills and stay on their good side.

Naturally, I was very eager to start meeting the people at the mills and was frustrated that I was left behind. So one day I said to Dudley, very casually, "How about taking me with you to the mills? I want to see how the steel is made and get to know the people."

I could see right away he was not receptive to the idea.

His answer was surprisingly candid. "Morris, you're the nephew. If you develop contacts with the people in the mills, your uncle may decide that he doesn't need *me* anymore."

"Dudley," I said, surprised, "I always work for *you*."

He wasn't buying it and didn't take me with him to the mill that day or any day for another couple of weeks. He did, however, bring up the subject a couple of times, saying things like, "So Morris, do you promise you won't take my job if I take you to the mills?" I always said the same thing: that Dudley was my superior and I worked for *him*; that I would never do anything to undermine him. And finally, the day came when he took me with him to the different mills and introduced me to the people there. He told them, "I'm going to give Morris some different responsibilities." I wasn't sure what he meant by that, but I was very happy to hear it.

Once I had been introduced to the people at the mills, one of my jobs was to go to the mills to pick up their surplus lists of overrun prime and rejects and waste that each mill was selling. This was long before computers, so the list was handwritten, and I had to go to a certain office at each mill on Mondays and ask for it. I'd bring the lists back to Dudley's office and put them on his desk, and later he would go over them to see which items might be worth buying, either to sell to customers immediately or to put in our warehouse for future sale.

In the process of picking up the lists, I would stop and chat with the people in their offices to get to know them. Some mills had friendlier people than others: Youngstown Sheet & Tube and Republic were friendly mills, while U.S. Steel seemed harder to break into. In the end, though, I got to know all of the people and made some good friends. I would have lunch with certain people when I came by for the lists; later, I occasionally went to dinner with them.

I picked up and studied these lists for about a month, observing Dudley as he studied them and decided which steel to buy. After about a month, when Dudley saw that I had developed some relationships at the mills, he said, "You can call on some of those mills. But before you go, let me know where you're going, and when you come back, let me know how you make out." And that's how I started buying steel for Allied on my own.

I began buying standard batches of steel that I knew would be easy to sell; in the steel business, we refer to these as "vanilla" items. But there was a catch: when the mill sold you prime steel, they also sold you some subprime steel. You had no choice; if you wanted the good material that was easy to sell, you had to buy some of the not-so-good stuff with it. Luckily, even the not-so-good stuff could be sold, back in those days.

Of course, it was inevitable that I would make mistakes. Steel is made up of many different elements, including iron, carbon, nickel, chromium, and manganese. Different alloys give the steel different properties, which make it useful for different purposes. If the steel doesn't have exactly the right composition, it can be worthless to the customer. I didn't understand this at first, so sometimes, when a load of steel I bought came in from the mills, Dudley would take one look at it and tell me that the company I'd intended it for couldn't use it. Then I'd have to scramble to find a new customer. I knew I had to educate myself about the chemical makeup of steel, so I bought some books on metallurgy that I found very hard to understand. I had never even finished high school: what did I know about chemistry or metallurgy? But I was doing business with college graduates at the mills who understood this and I knew I had to learn it. So I studied the books and kept searching for people who were willing to answer my questions.

Buying the wrong kind of steel was certainly not the only thing I did wrong. I still had to learn all kinds of things in order to be successful in business. To begin with, the way I dressed was all wrong, like wearing bright red socks with a blue suit. Dudley would frown at me and say, "You have to have a certain look when you deal with the mills, Morris. With a blue suit, you should always wear dark socks."

He also insisted that I stop eating like a European, with the fork permanently held in the left hand and the knife in the right.

"Eat like an American," he urged me. "Cut your food with the fork in your left hand and the knife in your right hand. Then lay the knife down on the edge of the plate and transfer the fork to your right hand for eating."

It was such an ordeal to keep shifting my fork from one hand to the other! I couldn't understand why Americans liked to eat that way. But, of course, Dudley was right. When in Rome, do as the Romans do. People feel more comfortable with you when you look and act the way they do. And in business, the more you're like the other guy, the easier it is to establish good relationships. And relationships are the fuel that drives making deals and doing business. If you can make the other guy feel comfortable with you and like you, you'll be a lot more likely to strike a deal.

Over time, Dudley allowed me to do more and more for him. In the beginning, he would watch me very carefully, listening in when I was dealing with someone over the phone or following up after I'd had a meeting, asking me to tell him exactly what happened. Then he would evaluate what I'd done and tell me what I'd done right and wrong. He was a good teacher and I was an eager student. I knew learning was essential if I wanted to be successful.

I took on more and more responsibilities, and several years later I was promoted to Vice President of Operations. In addition to making sure the plant ran well, I bought and sold a lot of steel for Allied. But even though I was continuously getting more sophisticated about steel, I was still a greenhorn in many ways. One time I met with a man from Milwaukee who came to my office and said, "I represent companies like John Deere that need steel. Unfortunately, they are having difficulty placing their orders with the mills, which is why I have come to you."

I nodded. "Thank you for thinking of us."

"My clients' needs are tremendous," he said, "and they are willing to pay top price for steel. They are also willing to show their gratitude if you can help them out."

With that, he opened a briefcase that was filled to the brim with stacks of money. He then took out a piece of paper, unfolded it and showed me a long list of company names and the kinds and quantities of steel they wanted.

"For each order you place with the mills on behalf of my clients, you will receive a generous cash bonus. A *personal* bonus."

Suddenly I understood: he was offering me money if Allied would put his clients' orders on the mills' books. I was intrigued by his offer, so I told him I would think about it and asked him to come back the following week.

Then I went to see Dudley and told him what happened. He just looked at me with amazement and shook his head. Finally, he said patiently, "Morris, what happens if you take money from this man but the mill won't accept the orders you promised to place for him? You took his money, but you can't deliver the steel. You will have a problem."

Once again, Dudley was right. So when the man from Milwaukee came back to my office the next week, I told him, "I can't take your orders because I can't guarantee delivery."

"Oh, that's not an issue," the man said easily. "I'm sure you can deliver."

"I can't make that guarantee."

"It won't be a problem."

"If I can't deliver, there might be problems."

"Nonsense. I'm a very honest businessman."

Honest? I thought. He's offering me a bribe; how honest can he be?

"Listen, it's possible that I won't be able to get the mills to take your orders."

"That's all right. I'm an honest businessman."

Over and over again, he kept telling me there would be no problems if I couldn't fulfill all the orders, because he was an honest businessman. And over and over, he told me he was "honest." He kept pushing until finally I'd had it. I stood up and said, "Listen, you're so lily white, you shouldn't be around me. I might contaminate you! Goodbye!"

I found out later that he was a "steel bootlegger" who went to people like me who had contacts with the mills and bribed them to get his clients' orders put on the mills' books. I wondered what happened if people took the bribe but didn't deliver. Did anyone get their legs broken?

I can say without reservation that Dudley was a great teacher. And one of the most important things he taught me was to watch what I said. This was something I really needed to be warned about because if I got angry, I sometimes said things I shouldn't. Obviously, that's not a good idea in business (or personal life, for that matter). It's not that I was nasty, but I was young and foolish, and my temper was sometimes hotter than it should have been.

One time I stormed into Dudley's office complaining about one of our customers.

"They're bitching about nothing! There's nothing wrong with the steel we sent them; they're just trying to get us to mark down the price. I'm going to call them up right now and tell them what a bunch of bastards they are!"

Dudley gave me a look that stopped me in my tracks.

"Whoa, just wait a minute there, Morris! Be careful what you say, because once you say it, it doesn't belong to you anymore."

I had never considered that, although it certainly seemed to be true. Once it's out there, you can't take it back. Then, when the steam finally stopped coming out of my ears, Dudley continued.

"Write them a letter and put that letter in a drawer for a week. After that, if you still feel the same way, you can send it."

I followed his advice and, naturally, a week later I threw the letter in the trash.

I truly appreciated Dudley's teaching and guidance, and still do to this day. He really helped to shape me as a businessman and, God knows, I needed it. In return, I was determined never to undermine him or try to take his position. That's why, when the two of us went to the Builder's Board of Directors meeting every quarter and reported on the activity at Allied or answered questions from other board members, I always made it clear that Dudley was in charge. If we were asked how a certain order was going and it was my turn to speak, I would say, "Dudley talked to the man at the mill, who said such-and-such." Often, even if a question was asked about a matter I was handling, I would say, "I have to refer that to Dudley; he can answer you." If you'd listened to me at those meetings, you would have thought that every deal we made was Dudley's deal. But years earlier I had promised Dudley that I was working for *him*, and I was determined never to go back on that promise.

What I didn't know was that Dudley had been quietly telling Uncle Jack that I was learning how to schmooze with people from the mills and deal with clients. He reported that I was developing contacts with new clients all around the country and taking on more and more of his duties. Yet Dudley never told me that he was paving the way for me to take over his job. He was a wonderful mentor and a true gentleman.

By the early 1950s, it became apparent that Dudley was no longer well. I could see that he was slowing down, taking longer and longer lunches and turning over more and more of his work to me. Soon I was doing maybe eighty percent of his work for him, including making many of the deals to buy and sell steel. My title was now Executive Vice President in Charge of Operations, but I was doing most of the president's work. Still, I felt the need to keep up the illusion that Dudley was fully in charge, and I was protective of him and his job. If Uncle Jack happened to call, for example, and Dudley was out having a very late lunch, I would say, "Dudley's at the mill, Uncle Jack. I'll try to get hold of him." And if Uncle Herman called to ask a question, I would say, "I'll ask Dudley and get back to you."

Eventually, though, Dudley got so tired and sick that he had to see a doctor, who did some tests and found out that he had colon cancer. Dudley went to the hospital in early December for an operation, and when he came home a few weeks later, he looked fine. I went to his house for a Christmas celebration, and we went to a board meeting in Cleveland a few weeks later. He seemed to be doing well during this trip and I was elated. But soon he was down and out again, and in 1952 he went into the hospital for the last time. When he died, I was truly devastated. I had lost not only a mentor but a true friend, and I miss him to this day.

CHAPTER SEVEN

President of Allied Metals

"Don't be silly," Uncle Jack said irritably, peering up at me over his glasses from behind a stack of paperwork. "A Jew cannot be president of Allied."

"Why not?" I shot back. "I've been doing the work of the president for a long time."

He sighed heavily.

"A Jew can do the *work* of president," he replied with exaggerated patience, "but he cannot *be* president."

Then he leaned back in his chair and folded his arms, signaling that the subject was closed.

Now that Dudley had passed away, the job of president was up for grabs. And I wanted it so bad I could taste it. I knew for a fact that I could do it. I'd been running the company for the few weeks that had passed since Dudley's death. And in large part, I'd been running it for years behind the scenes. So while my uncle may have thought the subject was closed, I did not, and I reminded him for the umpteenth time how qualified I was for the job.

"You *are* qualified," Uncle Jack agreed wearily. "Dudley has been telling me all along about what you were doing for him. But a Jew cannot be president."

"Why not?" I practically screamed, frustrated.

"Because, Morris, the mills are not so enamored of a Jewish company."

"Builder's is a Jewish company and the mills sell *you* steel," I countered, stunned at his lack of logic.

"But we only send *goys* to deal with the mills. If you were the president of Allied, you'd also be going to the mills. And that wouldn't work."

I couldn't believe my ears.

"Listen to me, Uncle Jack," I said, leaning over his desk. "I want to tell you something. I've been dealing with the people from the mills for years and they all know I'm Jewish. And guess what—they sell me steel anyway! We go drinking together, we golf together, we have dinner with the wives. The other wives love Phyllis and ask her advice on what clothes and shoes to buy. I have *never* seen anti-Semitism in this business. Just give me a chance!"

We went round and round for several days until finally a great miracle occurred—Uncle Jack agreed to make me president of Allied Metals!

"But I'll be watching you," he warned, shaking a finger at me.

And watch he did, like a hawk, along with Uncle Herman. The two of them went over every single thing I did for years. And the very first thing that happened almost cost me the job right then and there.

A little while before Dudley died, we had bought a press, a big machine that stamped pieces of steel into different shapes. We purchased the press from the government, installed it at Allied, and set it to work stamping high-strength cross beams for steel trailers, specifically for Freuhauf Trailer Company.

On a Monday, just as I was walking into my office around lunchtime, I noticed a group of about a dozen women lined up just outside the door. With them was the President of the Niles City Council. I invited everyone into my office, where the councilman announced, "These ladies are very upset because your press shakes their houses right down to the foundations. You'll have to turn off the press."

If we had to stop the press, we would lose a lot of money, a disaster in the making for my career. My uncle would say that I didn't know how to run the company and put someone else in my place. I had no idea what to do, so I told my visitors I'd get back to them, left the office, and went to a very nice restaurant and bar called the Café 422, one of Dudley's watering holes. I ordered a drink and then had lunch, all the while trying to figure out what I should do. Should I move the press? Buy up all the houses? Either option was way too expensive.

Suddenly, who should walk into the café but Carmen DeChristofaro, the very tall mayor of Niles. I knew him well because Allied always made a point of contributing to our local politicians. Also, when he wasn't acting as mayor, he worked for Republic Steel, a company we often did business with. (Being mayor was not a full-time job in Niles.)

"Hey, Morrie!" he said, shaking my hand and patting me on the shoulder like a true politician. "You look like you have a problem. What's wrong?"

"Aaah, you couldn't help me," I replied glumly.

"Tell me what's wrong anyway."

So I did. Carmen, of course, was well acquainted with the president of the City Council, and when I finished my tale of woe, he said, "That little guy always gives me a lot of problems. Let me see what I can do for you."

That afternoon, he called me at the office to set up a dinner meeting. And at that meeting, he waited until we'd finished our meal and were having a couple of drinks before announcing, "I've decided I'm going to help you. I'll come to your office Wednesday morning. You call the councilman and tell him to be there, with the ladies. Tell him you're going to fix whatever you can. But don't tell him I'll be there."

It was all very mysterious, but he refused to tell me more. Having nothing to lose, I agreed, and on Wednesday morning, the councilman and the ladies gathered in my office. The ladies were carrying on about how much the press was vibrating their houses when suddenly Mayor Carmen came in and said, "Ladies, thank you for coming. The councilman says the press is shaking your foundations and that's very distressing. But don't worry. I have city engineers outside, sitting in my car and I'm going to take them to each one of your houses. They will put meters in your basements so we can fully assess the situation."

The expressions on the women's faces changed from anger to a mixture of surprise and alarm. And the councilman looked shocked! I couldn't understand why they were so alarmed at the thought of meters. Noticing their reactions, the mayor reassured them, "This is important. We need to know how much your houses are shaking."

Suddenly the women began to murmur among themselves, shake their heads, and turn away. But the mayor assured them this was important.

"Oh, no, that's okay," one of them said.

"We don't need the meters," chimed in another.

"Of course you do," smiled the mayor. "Then we'll know exactly how much your houses are shaking."

But those women and the councilman just couldn't seem to get out of my office fast enough. They made a beeline for the door and were in their cars and pulling away in a matter of minutes! As it turned out, there was no shaking in those houses and the councilman knew it. He got the women to say there was a problem because he wanted Allied to pay him to go away—and he probably told the women there would be some money in it for them, too. Fortunately, the mayor was on to them and was willing to help me out. It's nice to have friends in high places!

Once I was fully in charge of running Allied, the company became more profitable than ever, I'm happy to say. Dudley was a very smart guy and had been a good president for many years, but during those last couple of years he'd gotten tired and his heart just wasn't in it. I don't blame him: everything must be a lot harder when cancer is eating you up from inside. But the steel business doesn't care if you're tired. You make good deals and produce profits, or you're finished.

Our goals at Allied were very simple. First, we had to get steel from the mills, whether the source was an overrun, an irregular batch that had been rejected, or one of our own orders. Second, we had to find customers who needed this steel, which wasn't difficult because lots of companies needed steel. That's why I was primarily focused on getting into the mills and making contacts, so we could buy the steel. Usually I would make an appointment and go introduce myself when I was trying to break into a new mill, but sometimes I made important contacts just by being lucky.

In the 1960s, my son, Steven, was attending Howe Military Academy in Howe, Indiana, and Phyllis and I used to visit him on family days or when other events were held. Naturally, we would meet other parents, and that was how I got acquainted with a man named Ed Murray. From the way he dressed and carried himself, Ed was obviously an important man. We got to know each other a little bit and he invited me to go golfing at the Klinger Country Club, which was near the school. We were pretty evenly matched; when we bet on a game, sometimes I would win ten bucks from him, and sometimes he would win the same amount from me. During our games, we talked about our sons or the school or the weather, but never discussed business.

One Monday, I had a lunch date with Keith Melton, Manger of Secondary Steel at U.S. Steel in Pittsburgh. Keith was the guy who decided whether or not I could buy irregular steel from the mill, and he had never been very generous to me. This particular

Monday I was sitting downstairs waiting to take Keith to lunch, when the elevator opened and out stepped Ed Murray, my golfing acquaintance.

He saw me right away and said, surprised, "What are you doing here?"

"I'm in the steel business."

"I never knew that."

"Well, we never talked business. I'm going to lunch with Keith Melton."

"No you're not."

Then he picked up the phone at the receptionist's desk and asked the operator to connect him with Mr. Melton's office.

"Keith, I'm taking Morris Friedman to the Duquesne Club for lunch." The Duquesne Club was a very private club—and restricted, to boot: Jews were not welcome. But that didn't seem to matter, since I was having lunch with Ed Murray, one of the top executives of U.S. Steel!

When we got back to Ed's office, he went one step further and called Keith Melton, telling him, "Morris is coming to see you. And I want you to treat him right."

In the past, Melton would only sell me a little bit of steel. But after that lunch, I became a favored customer.

Besides introducing myself or being introduced, a third way to get in with a steel mill was to do them a favor. This is the way I managed to connect with Wheeling Steel in Pittsburgh. I had called on them many times, never making much headway, until one day when they called me with a large amount of irregular steel that they wanted to get rid of. The steel was supposed to have been sold to a company that manufactured nails. But something was wrong with it, and the customer refused to take it. Since there were only a few companies that made nails, the mill would have a hard time selling it for anything more than scrap, which brought a very low price.

"Can you find a place for it?" the man from Wheeling asked.

I knew I didn't have many customers who could use this steel, but I told him I'd see what I could do. I made lots of calls to customers over the next couple of days, offering them the steel, but no one was interested. Then I realized that this steel could be used to make washers. That's what you do with very low-cost material—make washers.

I found a firm that was willing to buy it to make washers and, although there wasn't much profit to be made in the deal, went ahead and bought the steel from Wheeling at a very low price. But instead of taking delivery of it all at once, I had them stretch it out, so I was taking only so much this month, so much the next, and so on. That way, I could use the monthly payments I was getting from the customer to pay for the steel and didn't have to tie up my own money or borrow from the bank. I only made a few dollars on the deal, but because I did Wheeling a favor, they were much nicer to me from then on.

Our second goal at Allied, finding new customers, was obviously just as important as finding the steel. We couldn't rely on only a few customers buying from us over and over again, like people who go to the market to buy milk and eggs every week. And even if we could find customers like this, we didn't always get the type or quantity of steel from the mills that they needed. One day, for example, Republic Steel might sell us ten tons of 22-gauge prime with a composition that made it suitable for flat work. And the next day, U.S. Steel might sell us two tons of quarter-inch irregular that was better suited for being made into different products, once we'd cut away the poorly made sections, which were used for something else entirely. Each batch we received was different, and needed to be matched with the right customer.

Luckily, finding new customers wasn't that hard. We just kept calling around and meeting new people, and somehow always seemed to have someone to sell to. And often, customers looking for steel called *us*.

But finding steel and finding new customers weren't the only things we had to do. We still needed to make sure we had top-notch people working in our warehouse, plant, sales office, managers' offices, and everywhere else. Because no matter how much steel we got our hands on, if we didn't have good people facilitating the business, there would be trouble.

I was constantly on the lookout for some way to expand the business and make more money. And I finally found what I was looking for in a new kind of steel on the market called "coils." Up until then, the mills sold us steel in certain shapes: plates, bars, wires, I-beams, and so on. But then they began to sell it to us in a new shape, a coil that was made from very long sheets of very thin steel. Think of a roll of aluminum foil, the kind you use in your kitchen, lying on the counter. Now imagine a giant roll of this "foil," six feet wide and weighing several tons. That's what a coil of rolled steel is like. To use it, you unroll it partway, cut off a piece, and process it. You might, for example, put the steel into a pressing machine to stamp out car parts.

The mills produced wide coils because they were more profitable. And some of their customers wanted wide coils. But other customers needed something narrower, perhaps three feet wide, or 17.6 inches wide, or maybe only 3.5 inches wide. Naturally, the mills didn't want to waste time and money making coils in different widths for each customer: that was too costly and time-consuming. But that created a moneymaking opportunity for us. There was a giant machine called a "slitter" that would unwind the coil from one end and cut the sheet of steel into different widths as it passed through the machine. Then it would rewind everything on the other end. It was sort of like slicing a wide lasagna noodle into three different sizes—fettuccini, spaghetti, or angel hair pasta—then rolling them all up separately.

I got excited when I found out about the slitters and talked it up to Uncle Jack and Uncle Herman. If we bought one for Allied, we could start with a coil that was, say, six feet wide, run it through the slitter and end up with four narrower coils, each with a different width: say, 30 inches, 22 inches, 14.5 inches, and 5.5 inches. Each of the four coils would be cut to the exact dimensions needed by the customer. Uncle Jack agreed that it sounded like a good opportunity, so I bought a slitter for Allied—our first one. This made us the first warehouse to have one (at least as far as I knew), and, right from the start, that machine made money for us.

The late 1950s and early 1960s were good years for us at Allied, with the slitter bringing in lots of new revenue and increased profit, but Builder's was struggling. Near the end of one year, I went to Cleveland for a meeting of the Board of Directors, during which we went through statements from the accountants, talked about our strategies for the coming year, and had standard board meeting discussions. Then Uncle Jack, who was Chairman of the Board, informed me that when I got back to Allied, I would have to tell my people that there would be no bonuses for them this year.

This surprised me. Bonuses were always given when the company had a good year, and the employees expected them. They were good for morale and gave the employees incentive to work harder. It didn't make sense that Allied was getting nothing after such a stellar year.

"Why no bonuses?" I asked. "We had a good year. My people deserve bonuses."

"You had a good year," Uncle Jack acknowledged. "But *we* had a bad one. We need the money to sustain the business."

This stung me to the quick. "How can I *not* give my people bonuses when we had a good year!?"

The room went silent and nobody moved. But I was not going to let this one go.

"I won't do it!" I exclaimed as I rose to my feet.

To stand up to Uncle Jack like this was unheard of, especially in front of other people. But I didn't care; I had to speak my mind.

"Sit down," Uncle Jack said evenly, although his face was getting redder by the minute.

Thank God, one of the men on the board, Tommy Thompson, who was V.P. of Sales for Builder's, was brave enough to say, "Mr. Friedman, I think you should hear your nephew out."

Uncle Jack agreed but folded his arms, which was not a good sign. I repeated that my people had done very well this year and deserved their bonuses. And if we weren't able to give bonuses to certain key employees, there was a good chance they might quit and go to work for someone else.

This didn't impress Uncle Jack in the least. So I told him I was going to go back to Allied and tell my people, "Allied made money this year, but Builder's didn't, so the board at Builder's decided there would be no bonuses for anyone."

I went back to Allied and told them exactly that, adding, "This is not fair and I'm very sorry. If you stay with me, I'll make it up to you later. If you don't, that's your choice." Fortunately (for me and for Allied), most of the employees stayed. But we did lose some, including some very good salesmen, and there was nothing I could do about it.

In the meantime, there was another money problem brewing. Even though I had climbed all the way up the ladder at Allied, I was not making as much money as you might think. I received a fairly nice salary, but it was nothing compared to the salaries of presidents of similar companies. And even though I was President of Allied and a member of the Board of Directors for Builder's, Uncle Jack never gave me any stock in either company, or any of the other steel companies that Builder's owned. Having stock in Builder's would have made me part-owner of a pretty nice business. But Uncle Jack was not in the habit of giving away stock, as he wanted to keep complete control of the company.

Frustrated by this situation, I went to his office and made an announcement.

"Uncle Jack, I make nice profits at Allied every year and lots of money is transferred to Builder's. It's time for me to get a raise."

"I agree, Morris," he sighed. "But I have a lot of nephews and grandchildren and cousins working for me. If I give you a raise, I'll have to give them all raises."

What a silly argument, I thought. "No, you don't have to give them all raises. Nobody has to know what I'm making."

"There are family members in the accounting department at Allied," he reminded me. "Everyone will know."

"Well, who cares if they know?

"Morris," he said, "I have to do a lot of things for family. Giving you a raise, but not them, will cause lots of problems."

I wasn't going to be put off so easily. After much persuasion, I finally got Uncle Jack to agree that I would get a commission on every sale made at Allied. But the money wouldn't be transferred from the customer to Allied to me, because then the family would know. Instead, I created my own little company and from that point on, companies who hired Allied to do their steel slitting actually did business with *both* Allied and my company. And when it was time to pay their bills, they wrote two checks: a large one to Allied, and a much smaller one, a commission check, to my company.

On Fridays, I would drive up to Cleveland to square things with Uncle Jack. I'd hand him invoices and other papers showing the transactions we'd completed and how much money I had received through my company. It always took a while before he was satisfied, because his eyesight wasn't very good and he had trouble reading the papers. He would ask me question after question, often the same ones from different angles, to see if he could trip me up. But he was always satisfied in the end because I believed in playing fair and he could see that. To me, a deal is a deal; once I agree to something, I never try to make extra by cheating. I always knew when he was satisfied because he would hand the papers back to me and say, "You make sure you pay your taxes on this."

Naturally, I was very happy to be making extra money through my company, but, as Uncle Jack had predicted, the rest of the family was not. All of those nephews and grandchildren and cousins working for the company were aware that I was making more money. And even if they didn't know about my company, they were suspicious. Many of them thought I was stealing from the company and cheating Uncle Jack, which, of course, was the furthest thing from the truth. But neither Uncle Jack nor I would say anything about my "side deal" because then everyone else would want one of their own.

After a couple of years of doing business this way, I started to become unhappy with the arrangement. I didn't like hiding behind anything, even if it was completely honest. Instead, I asked Uncle Jack to give me a raise or give me a commission on all the steel I sold. But he wouldn't do it. Things finally came to a head when I bought a second slitter but told Uncle Jack I wasn't going to install it at Allied until we made a new deal.

"Why?" he asked me, with a hurt look on his face. "Aren't you happy?"

"I'm very happy working for you, but I don't like when certain members of the family call me a thief and say other mean things about me. Even Uncle Herman is telling people I'm a thief."

Uncle Jack just waved me off. "Don't worry about Herman. He flops around like a fly in buttermilk."

"I don't want the family saying bad things about me," I persisted.

"All right. What can we do?"

"No more side deals," I said firmly.

I could now speak to him that way because Allied was the most profitable part the company, and Builder's was not doing as well.

"I want my money to come to me directly."

"Okay," Uncle Jack said, throwing up his hands. "What do you want?"

"For every ton we slit, I want a dollar paid to me from Allied, in the open, where everyone can see."

We went back and forth a little before settling on fifty cents per ton. I asked Uncle Jack to write a memo to the Treasurer of Allied Metals spelling out our deal, and from then on I got my fifty cents per ton. While fifty cents may not sound like a lot of money, we were slitting thousands and thousands of tons every year, and fifty cents went a lot further in those days than it does now. So I was happy, although not rich, because even with the extra money, I was still not making what people in my position at other companies could make. But Uncle Jack just kept saying, "Don't worry, Morris. I'll take care of you. You'll see, I'll take care of you."

Although my uncle and I had a rather tempestuous relationship, we grew closer over the years. After Aunt Ethel died and he married his second wife, Madeline, Phyllis and I began spending a lot of time with the two of them as a foursome, and every Friday we would drive to Cleveland to have dinner with them. As I got a little older and shouldered more and more responsibility, I began to understand Uncle Jack better. He had come to this country with nothing, just a few pennies in his pocket, and built a big company from scratch. He then spent a great deal of money getting the family out of Europe, both before and during the Holocaust, and put many of us on the payroll or took care of us in different ways. I had a lot of admiration and respect for him.

By 1968, I could see that Uncle Jack was definitely feeling his age and slowing down. He walked with a cane and had his share of medical problems, including an enlarged heart. Although he went to work every day, he no longer had the energy to supervise a company like Builder's and watch his people carefully, a situation that always leads to trouble.

It was around this time that Uncle Jack asked me to sell, then ship, three thousand tons of Allied steel to Builder's at a low price, which was a perfectly legal way of transferring money from one company to the other. Evidently he was having some trouble with the bank and needed to make his books look better, which was fine with me. So Allied sold the steel to Builder's very cheaply, just covering costs, and I assumed that Builder's was going to sell it elsewhere at the going rate and make a nice profit. Or maybe they were going to leave the steel on the books for a while for tax purposes. I didn't know what the plans were.

Later that same day, I got a call from a fellow who worked in a high position at Builder's. He said, "Don't actually ship the steel to us; just write the sale down on the books."

I knew this was a bad move, even though what he said made sense from a financial point of view. Shipping three thousand tons of steel from Niles to Cleveland is very expensive. If we just transferred the steel on the books and left it in Allied's warehouse, Builder's would save a lot of money on freight charges. But doing that would be absolutely illegal. When a subsidiary sells steel to its parent company, the steel *has* to be put on trucks and moved to the purchaser. And there must be shipping documents to prove it.

"Are you crazy?" I shot back. "What about the shipping documents?"

"Go ahead and fill out the shipping documents, but don't ship anything. We're just trying to make our books look better."

I couldn't believe it. Now he was telling me to commit a second crime by falsifying shipping documents.

"No. I won't do that. We could go to jail!"

I blame this incident on the fact that Uncle Jack was no longer keeping tabs on every part of the business. When the big boss is not checking invoices himself, walking through the plant every day, asking employees what's happening in their departments, talking to the people at the mills and the customers, watching the trucks come in and out of the warehouse and so on, there are too many ways for people to stir up trouble. They make mistakes, take shortcuts, become overly eager, or get lazy and do something that could spell disaster for everyone involved. Even if everyone working for you is perfectly honest, you have to keep checking up on everything and everybody.

Uncle Jack wasn't checking up on much anymore. People were not working as hard as they should have, at least one that I knew of was doing illegal things, and some were helping themselves to Uncle Jack's money. I saw this myself when he sent a grandson to me, asking me to take him to the mills and introduce him to the people there. "I want him to learn more about the business," Uncle Jack explained.

So I took the grandson to the mills, introduced him to everyone, and took him with me when I had drinks and dinner with various people from the mills. I paid for everything from my Allied expense account: all the dinners, the drinks, the cigars, everything. A little later, when I went to Cleveland for a weekend, I spent some time at Builder's. The door to the grandson's office happened to be open, so I went in and saw, on his desk, an expense report for entertainment during the days he went with me to the mills. I couldn't believe it! That little "B" hadn't spent a penny! This may seem like a small thing, a little expense account padding, but it's like rot in a tree. It starts small but it spreads, and one day the whole tree comes crashing down.

Builder's, like a rotten tree, was being eaten up from the inside by bad employees. There were also too many bad deals, and the company owed lots of money to the mills—so much, in fact, that the mills were threatening to stop selling them steel. If that happened, Builder's would be finished. The bank was also starting to poke its nose into Builder's business because of heavy debts.

Something drastic needed to be done, and Uncle Jack knew it. At this point he quietly began the process of adopting me as his son, which he thought would help ensure that the company would remain strong once he passed on. He had no son of his own, only two daughters. He told his attorney to prepare the papers, and the attorney, to make sure there could be no legal challenge later on, suggested that Uncle Jack see a psychiatrist and get a report saying he was of sound mind when he adopted me. Unfortunately, it never came to pass. His heart suddenly gave out one Saturday night while he was sitting in his living room.

When I heard he was gone, I felt like my own father had died.

CHAPTER EIGHT

The Best Fifty Bucks

I never mourned the death of my father, Aba Zalke.

My final memory of him dates back to when I was fifteen years old and sitting on a train in Prague, just about to leave for France, where I'd board the ship that would take me to America. As my train pulled away, I could see my father standing on the platform with my sister, waving and waving, a tear running down his cheek. I waved back, until finally the two of them disappeared in a cloud of smoke. It was only a few years later that he disappeared forever in another cloud of smoke, released from this Earth through a crematorium chimney in a Nazi death camp. I never really had the chance to grieve for him, or for my mother and two younger brothers, who were also killed by the Nazis. It was almost as if these deaths had never happened. They all just disappeared at some point—I never knew exactly when.

Perhaps because of this, when my Uncle Jack died, I mourned as if he had been my father. And in some ways, he was. He had saved my life and provided me with a fresh start by bringing me to the United States. He welcomed me into his family and gave me the means to support myself. He mentored me and allowed me to rise as far as I could in the business, although he made me fight every step of the way. But that was good because it made me stronger. Yes, he did some foolish things, but who among us is perfect? He could drive me crazy sometimes, and there were times when I was very angry with him, but I always loved and admired him.

"I feel so bad," I said to Phyllis as we drove to Cleveland for the funeral. "I feel like I lost my father."

"No," she corrected me. "He was never a father to you—*you* were like a son to *him*."

While Phyllis and Aunt Madeline were at Uncle Jack's apartment, I suddenly decided that I needed to see Uncle Jack. I couldn't really believe that he had passed away, and I needed to see him for the final time. Phyllis said she would go with me, but I replied, "Not this trip. I have to go by myself," and went to the funeral home alone. When I saw him lying there, he looked so small. He had always been larger than life, and now he seemed impossibly small. An autopsy had been performed because he had died so suddenly, and you could see the thick sutures that had been used to close the opening in the back of his head and neck. It gave me an eerie feeling.

Uncle Jack's departure left a big empty space in my heart, and a huge vacuum that needed to be filled at Builder's. Everyone at Builder's knew that big changes were in store, but no one knew what those changes might be. There was no plan in place for succession because Uncle Jack simply hadn't made one, even in the midst of planning to adopt me. The only thing that was certain was that the bank served as executor of Uncle Jack's will. The bank executives panicked because Builder's owed them a huge sum of money; if the company went under, the bank would take a huge financial hit. They wanted to install a new CEO right away, but none of Builder's current executives were ready to take charge. Uncle Jack had held fast to his power right up until the end and hadn't prepared anyone to take his place. Knowing the role I had played at Allied, Mr. Meyers, the bank's vice president, asked me if I would care to move over to the parent company and run Builder's.

"I'll run *both* companies, Builder's and Allied," I replied, confidently. "Let's make a contract."

This may sound like a very cocky thing to say, but I really believed in myself. I knew what I had done in the past and had a clear idea of what I could accomplish in the future. There was no doubt in my mind.

After a few conversations with Mr. Meyers and plenty of negotiation with the steel mills over past due bills, I finally got the bank and the mills to agree. The mills would continue to sell us steel on credit, and the bank would continue to give us loans so we could cover our expenses. I would take over as CEO of Builder's and continue as president of Allied, while overseeing all other subsidiaries. In exchange, I would receive a very nice salary plus two percent of the stock per year in Builder's, Allied, and the other companies Builder's owned. After five years, my interest would escalate to ten percent. It was a very good deal for me; I would be given a free hand to run the company as I saw fit and would be well compensated. The bank must have also seen it as a good deal, as they wanted me to sign the contract and take over as soon as possible.

While all of this negotiating and planning was going on, I was acting head of Builder's, and the more I looked into things, the more I realized the company was in big trouble. One of the first things I did was deal with our faulty equipment problem. Our high lifts and cranes were constantly breaking down and stopping all work in the plant. I soon found out that all of this equipment had been leased from an outfit in Chicago that was no longer servicing it. And why not? Because Builder's hadn't been making the lease payments due to cash shortages. I called the Chicago company and gave them a carrot-and-stick proposition. For the carrot, I promised to start making the lease payments immediately, which I did. And for the stick, I told them to either send someone to fix the equipment today or I would get it fixed myself and send them the bill. It worked, and we had far fewer equipment problems after that.

There was another issue I knew I needed to look into right away: a missing 1,000 tons of steel. Builder's had purchased a lot of 36-inch-wide hot roll coils of steel from Jones & Laughin Steel. The steel was actually a little wider than 36 inches when it arrived at Builder's plant. This was standard procedure; the mills were allowed to make this kind of steel about an inch wider, and we knew we would have to shave off the excess. We had special devices called scrap ballers that grabbed ahold of the thin slices of steel being shaved off the sides as the steel went through the slitters. This excess steel was "balled up" and set aside to be sold as scrap.

Unfortunately, there was a 1,000-ton difference between what the steel weighed when it was shipped from Jones & Laughin and what it weighed once it was slit and stacked on the factory floor, even accounting for the inch that was shaved off the sides. I went through all the paperwork, all the orders, shipping bills, and receipts, but couldn't figure out where the missing 1,000 tons had gone. This was a serious matter, because that missing steel had cost Builder's $100,000, which was a large amount of money back then—especially for a company having a difficult time turning a profit.

Unable to solve the problem in the office, I went down to the plant floor, where they were working on some of this very steel. As I watched as the men putting coils of steel through the slitter, I noticed something strange: the scrap ballers were having difficulty keeping up with the material being slit off the slides.

I asked the men operating the slitter to stop and measure the steel. What a surprise! The coils weren't 37 inches wide, which was the maximum allowed. They were 38, 39, and even 40 inches wide!

The mill had been shipping—and billing for—overly wide steel. (Steel was priced according to weight, so extra-wide coils meant extra weight and extra cost to us.) I ran a quick mental calculation and figured that much of the missing 1,000 tons was in the excess material the scrap ballers had been struggling with. Hurrying back to the office, I instructed one of the clerks to do a more careful calculation. His figures agreed with mine: most of the missing steel lay in those extra inches!

Why had Jones & Laughin been making overly wide steel? It may have been accidental. Or, just as likely, somebody was doing it on purpose so they could sell a lot of extra steel—remember, it was sold by weight—and make their "bogie," or bonus. And Builder's was paying for this excess steel, which became scrap.

I called Jones & Laughin and explained the situation, and just like that, the charge for most of that extra 1,000 tons went away.

For a couple of weeks after Uncle Jack died, I would get up at 3:00 a.m. to drive from Niles to Cleveland so I could get a lot of work done at Builder's before returning to Niles and Allied. And every single day, before I headed back to Niles, I would stop at the cemetery in Cleveland and sit on a bench by Uncle Jack's grave. This little ritual lasted only for a little while, but it was very peaceful there and I found it comforting.

I was working hard, but I was very happy knowing that I would soon be permanently in charge of both companies. Years earlier, I had told Uncle Jack I wanted to be the head of a big company, and finally it was going to happen. And then the roof caved in. The day I was supposed to sign the contract, I got a phone call from Mr. Meyers.

"You've got a crazy family," he informed me, sounding angry and frustrated. "They're calling a meeting and there's going to be problems."

Here we go, I thought. I put on my best suit, took a deep breath, and left for the meeting that would decide my fate. But I wasn't really all that worried, because even though my family could be a little *meshugenah* (crazy), I knew I deserved to be CEO. And who else would be able to do the job as well as I could? When all was said and done, I was pretty sure the family would agree that I was the best choice.

When I arrived at the bank, I was taken to a conference room in the back where I met with Mr. Meyers, Uncle Herman, and Uncle Jack's daughters (who were his heirs and now owned all of his stock). From the start, the atmosphere was very tense. As Mr. Meyers went over the terms of my proposed contract, Uncle Jack's daughters (my cousins) sat stiffly with no expression on their faces, almost like statues. It suddenly occurred to me that Mr. Meyers wasn't presenting my case with much confidence, although I didn't know why. Then, after we had listened to him for about ten minutes, one of Uncle Jack's daughters stood up and announced tersely, "We're having a stockholders meeting in a different room."

I was not a stockholder, but everyone else was. So everybody, including Mr. Meyers, got up and walked out, leaving me sitting there by myself.

After I'd been sitting there for maybe twenty minutes, the group returned and one of them, speaking for the others, gave me the verdict.

"You can run Builder's, but under our supervision. Your salary in this contract is acceptable to us, but we will only give you stock in Builder's, not in any of the other companies."

This hit me like a ton of bricks! In other words, I would be a hired man, not an owner. I would be told what to do by people who did not understand the steel business nearly as well as I did. And the only stock I would get would be Builder's, the worst performing of all the companies. No stock at all in Allied or the other companies that were doing well. The bottom line was this: because my cousins owned most of the stock, they had the power. And there was nothing I could do about it.

For the first time since Vasil yanked my *payos* and kicked me as I lay on the ground, I felt utterly defeated. I had worked in the family steel business for decades, since I was sixteen years old. I didn't know anything else. And now, it was either take this lousy deal or get out. I didn't respond to their offer; I just told them I would think about it and left as quickly as possible.

I felt as low as I ever had during the drive back to Niles. Once I got home, I dragged myself into the house and poured myself a drink. My son, Steven, now fifteen years old, was sitting in the living room doing his homework. He looked up and saw immediately that I was pretty down and out.

"Hi, Dad," he said. "So what happened?"

I hesitated for a minute, wondering if I should burden him with my problems. Then I decided he was old enough to understand. And I definitely needed someone to talk to. So I gave him the basics of the situation.

"I've had a beautiful job there," I concluded. "How can I leave? But how can I stay with the conditions they're offering?"

Steven may have been young, but he'd always been wise beyond his years. He said simply, "Things will get better for you." And when I later told Phyllis what had happened, she agreed with our son.

During the following days, I went in to work at Allied, but I was so depressed I could only go through the motions. Little did I know, there were people out there who were willing to extend themselves and be kind to me in my hour of need. They would help me make the decision to go out on my own, and then help me succeed once I got there.

The first one was my friend Carl Summers, the Treasurer at Youngstown Sheet and Tube. I went to see him at his office and told him what had happened. As I ran through my whole story, he sat at his desk motionless—so still I thought he wasn't listening to me. But once I finished, he started asking me all kinds of questions, like, "What exactly did they say about the stock?" and "Why do they want to oversee you?"

Carl knew about the original deal I had been offered by the bank, and once I'd answered all of his questions, he shook his head and summed up the situation, saying, "They're not doing right by you."

Then he looked me straight in the eye and said, "Leave them."

"How could I leave?" I asked, stunned at the thought.

"You're smart. You'll figure something out."

I knew Carl was right about not accepting the deal; I'd be hogtied and miserable. And although leaving the family business terrified me, as soon as Uncle Jack died, I had thought for a minute about leaving Allied and starting my own company. If the family doesn't make me a good offer, I'd said to myself, I'll leave. Of course, that was just an idle notion. I really wanted to stay, because running Builder's and the other companies was the job

I'd dreamed about since I was a teenager—one that could make me very rich.

"I'll tell you what," Carl continued. "If you go out on your own, I'll support you with credit. Now, I can't guarantee that we'll sell you any steel, because that's not my department. But if we do, I'll give you credit."

Extending credit to a company that didn't even exist yet was unheard of!

"I'm not worried," Carl said confidently. "I know you're honorable. So ...how much do you want?"

Stunned, all I could say was, "I don't know."

He smiled, probably because he had never seen me at a loss for words before. Then he told me how much credit his company would be willing to give me, adding, "And if you do well, we'll give you more next year."

I thought things over for a day or two, then called Mr. Meyers at the bank and told him I would not be taking over Builder's. In fact, I was resigning from Allied and walking away from everything, effective in two weeks.

"Oh, no, no, no, don't do that, Morris," he begged. "Take some time off, go fishing for a few weeks, then come back and we'll talk."

"No," I said firmly, utterly convinced I was doing the right thing.

"That's how you feel now, and that's understandable. But give it some time. It's a good job."

Of course Mr. Meyers wanted me back; the bank wanted me to rescue their investment. But I'd had enough. I called the mills that I had negotiated with during the previous few weeks and told them the deals we had made were off because I was leaving the company. And at the end of my last two weeks at Allied, I looked around the little office where I'd spent so many years, and I made the decision to leave without regret. A new life awaited me. I took some pictures off the wall and packed up a few things from my desk, including my "little black book," which held the names of all my contacts. It had taken me years to build up all those contacts, and even though there was a chance that I wouldn't be working in the steel business anymore, I couldn't bear to part with it.

So there I was, in my late forties, out of a job for the first time in thirty years. I had about $80,000 sitting in the bank, which meant I could feed my family for a while, but it was nowhere near enough to get established in the steel business. It cost millions of dollars to buy the machines, get a warehouse, hire people, and purchase steel to sell. Eighty thousand dollars wasn't even enough to stay in business for one day.

Despite this huge obstacle, I started calling people and telling them I was no longer with Allied and was interested in making deals on my own. A lot of them were surprised that I was walking away from a sure thing, even though I was being offered a bad deal; it seemed awfully risky. And it was.

Another kindness occurred on my very last day at Allied, when I called a man named Eddie Connors at U.S. Steel to talk about the possibility of buying steel from him for my new business.

He said he had some steel he might be able to sell me, but refused to tell me anything about it.

"Why won't you tell me about it?" I asked.

"Hang your shingle out first," he replied. "Then I'll tell you."

I didn't realize that he was protecting me. If we had made a deal involving my nonexistent company while I was still at Allied, I could be sued, and would probably lose.

A third kindness was extended to me by my friend Stanley Wilder, who owned a steel pickling business, when he offered me the free use of an empty room in his plant for my office.

"It's not much," he said with a shrug. "But you can set up a desk, put in a telephone, and you'll be back in business."

So I hauled in a flimsy old desk and set up an orange crate on its side for a chair. One person from Allied, Don Ray, joined me as Chief Financial Officer, and even though there were other people from Allied who asked to come with me, there was no way I could afford them. So there I was running a brand-new company that consisted of one boss, one employee, one telephone line, and one battered desk, all crammed into a borrowed office. We did have a grand name: United Steel Service. But we were in the crazy position of attempting to buy steel we simply couldn't afford. And if we did manage to get our hands on some, we couldn't fabricate, stamp, or slit the steel, because we had no machinery. But I couldn't focus on what we didn't have or couldn't do.

Right away I started buying and selling steel, but only in very small amounts. Tiny amounts. I had to be very careful, because I had no bank line of credit to fall back on and couldn't afford to make a single mistake. And slowly but surely, I began to make a few dollars here and a few dollars there. I was just starting to feel hopeful about the future when I received an official letter from my cousins' attorney: they were suing me for taking my little black book of contacts! According to my cousins, the address book belonged to Allied and contained proprietary information I was not entitled to have.

That was one of the lowest points in my life: I sank into a depression and sat around the house not knowing what to do. Even when Eddie Connors from U.S. Steel called to tell me he could sell me 100 tons of excess narrow-coil steel at a terrific price, I remained depressed. I went ahead and bought the steel, of course, but just let it sit in the U.S. Steel warehouse. Letting it sit was dangerous, for I needed to sell that steel as soon as possible to cover what I owed U.S. Steel. But I had no energy, no drive. I went to see Carl Summers again, and told him about the steel Eddie Connors had sold me.

"So what's wrong?" Carl asked.

"I don't know," I said, slumping down in my chair and shaking my head. "I just can't make myself go get that steel."

"Go see a psychiatrist," Carl said—it was practically an order. Then he reached into his desk drawer, took out a psychiatrist's business card and handed it to me.

I didn't think I needed a psychiatrist, but later that day I called and made an appointment with the shrink, figuring it couldn't hurt. I don't know what I expected him to do. I guess I thought he would ask me questions about my mother and uncover some subconscious conflict that had caused me to offend my cousins.

But once I settled into his office, the first thing he said to me was, "Tell me what you do."

I told him how I bought and sold steel, had learned the business from the bottom up, and made a lot of money for my uncle. I went through the whole story and rattled on for about forty minutes while he listened without commenting. Finally, when I was finished, he said calmly, "If you're telling me the truth, you should be able to do the same thing for yourself that you did for your uncle. Push ahead with your company."

"Do you know how hard it is to start with no money?" I moaned. "And besides, my cousins are suing me for taking my book of contacts."

The psychiatrist was unimpressed.

"Everybody gets sued," he replied indifferently. "Don't worry about that. Just get out there and do what you do. But this time, do it for yourself. Don't forget: When it rains no one holds the umbrella for you."

And it was as if a light bulb had been switched on in my head. All of a sudden I felt like I really could do it for myself!

The psychiatrist obviously felt he had done his job, because he then dismissed me with, "That will be $50, Mr. Friedman. And don't come back."

It turned out to be the best fifty bucks I ever spent.

The next day I went to the U.S. Steel mill in Gary, Indiana, to pick up the steel. It was a cold day in early April, and I stood there shivering as I supervised the loading of a hundred tons of steel—which had cost me $100,000 that I didn't have. As soon as the steel was loaded on the trucks, off it went to companies in Muncie, Indiana and Chicago and Joliet in Illinois. I made it a point to arrive at some of these companies at the same time the steel was delivered and offered a discount if they paid me right then, if they put a check in my hand before I left the building. Some did. And then I went back to my little office with the orange crate chair and showed the paperwork to my one trusty employee, Don Ray. He tallied up all of the expenses and announced that we had made a $40,000 profit.

It wasn't all that much, but to me it was everything.

Soon after that, a salesman from Allied named Ned Davis came to see me. I had no idea what he wanted; we couldn't afford to buy anything from Allied. He sat down in my little office and told me that the bank in Cleveland had finally hired someone to run Allied, a man named Bill Wolford. Ned said he had gone into Wolford's office to introduce himself and had asked his new boss, "So how do you spell your name?"

"You'll see it at the bottom of your paycheck," Wolford replied gruffly.

Ned, who had a short temper, found this offensive and snapped, "I'll never see *your* name on my paycheck!"

Now he sat on an orange crate in my office and said, "I want to work for you."

"I can't afford to pay you," I told him, shaking my head.

"You don't have to pay me," he replied, "until you have some money."

This was very good for me, because Ned had always been a great salesman, and, as it turned out, a lot of his accounts from Allied followed him to my new company. Things were definitely looking up. We had a line of credit at Youngstown Sheet and Tube, we had closed our first big deal, and I had both a financial wizard and a great salesman on my staff. I was still sitting on an upended orange crate in a borrowed office, with no warehouse, no machinery, and no line of credit at the bank—a line of credit was an absolute must in my business. But I felt as if I'd been reborn.

CHAPTER NINE

Kicked Out, Starting Over

Although it didn't seem like it at the time, getting pushed out of the family business was a wonderful thing for me. Like so many things in life, what seemed like the end of the world turned out to be only the beginning. Sitting on that orange crate in my tiny office, I was doing the same things I'd done at Allied—wheeling and dealing—with one important difference: I was working for myself. I made one deal after another, sometimes earning a big profit, sometimes a small one, and sometimes even losing a bit. But that's the way it is in the steel business, or any business, and overall I did pretty well.

However, I was worried about the lawsuit filed by Builder's, with Uncle Herman and my cousins behind it. They were accusing me of a lot of terrible things, including stealing money from Builder's through my "side deals" and the extra pay I got for slitting steel. Their lawyer made some very nasty threats—that is, until I produced a letter and a memo, each of which was clearly signed by Uncle Jack. The letter said:

Dear Nephew Morris:

Some of our relatives have said that you were making commissions from Allied operations. I know the facts in connection with all of these deals and they have been done with my full knowledge and consent.

Anyone who has been in the steel business as long as I have knows the facts of life and that sometimes [things] must be done to satisfy everyone and still keep the big end of the profit. I do appreciate what you have been able to do for Allied in the various matters. Any extra commissions which you received were meant to be in addition to your salary and represented many hours of extra work by you...

The memo, which was addressed to the Treasurer of Allied Metals, said:

Effective February 1, 1965, added compensation shall be paid to Morris Friedman of fifty cents ($0.50) per net ton on all tonnage slit on the 66" Paxton Slitter located at the Warren Plant of The Allied Metals Company. This will be effective until further notice.

As soon as my attorney showed these two documents to my cousins' lawyer, attitudes changed, the lawsuit became more casual, and the stress eased. I was able to turn my full attention to the business. One day I was visiting Carl Summer, the gentleman at Youngstown Sheet and Tube who had given me credit before my company was up and rolling. Later, he had also asked Bob

Williams, the president, to sell me steel. As I was sitting in Carl's office on this particular day, Bob happened to come by and we chatted a bit. Afterwards, he called an underling who was in charge of secondary steel and told him to make sure that Youngstown Sheet and Tube sold me *at least* 150 tons of steel a month. It wasn't a huge amount, but to have a guaranteed order like this was very nice. Favors like this were what helped my company get started and stay afloat. And, frankly, I don't know what I would have done without guys like Carl and Bob lending me a helping hand.

Bit by bit United Steel Service grew, and within a few years, I was able to hire more employees and buy a good-sized piece of land in Brookfield, Ohio, that was not far from Niles. There, I built my very own warehouse and plant, installing a "Cincinnati slitter" and a packing machine. My nephew Mel Moss, a graduate engineer from Case Western Reserve University, helped build the warehouse and install the machinery. A few years later, I expanded the plant, hired even more employees, and purchased more slitting machines. Still later, I added machines called burning tables and equipment to process structural steel. I now competed directly with Allied and Builder's, trying to buy steel from the same mills. It was competition on a grand scale—and I loved it!

For many years, I did very well by buying what is known as rejected steel. This is not irregular steel, which the mills realize is imperfect as soon as it's made. It's actually worse—or at least a bigger headache for the mills—because rejected steel is sold and shipped as a first-rate product. It only becomes rejected when the customer discovers it's not right, *after* it's been delivered.

When this kind of situation occurred, a mill would call and tell me that a customer in such-and-such a city had rejected a load of steel, and then ask if I wanted to buy it. And, just as important, they would ask if the steel could be shipped from the unhappy customer directly to our warehouse, so the mill wouldn't have to bring it back to their mill, store it, and ship it a second time, all of which was very expensive. This one phone call to me could solve all of their problems: I could buy the steel, pay for the shipping, and store it in my own warehouse. And it was usually a good deal for me because they sold me the steel at cut-rate prices.

In such cases, I usually wanted to inspect the steel before I committed myself, so I would go to the customer's plant, take a look at it, and, in many cases, buy it. But if the mill could tell me enough about the steel in advance, I would sometimes buy the steel without looking at it. This usually worked out fine, but occasionally there were unpleasant surprises.

One day I got a call from Republic Steel telling me that a General Motors plant in a nearby state had rejected a shipment, and asking if I was interested in buying it. From their description, I could tell it was actually good-quality steel (it might have been rejected by GM for very specific technical reasons), so I agreed to buy it and asked that it be shipped from the GM plant to our warehouse. Once it arrived, my shop foreman, Bobby Grexa, set his men to unloading the steel and breaking it into smaller bundles, and I came out to take a look.

When Bobby saw me, he smiled and said, "I see you were in Chicago."

Why in the world would he think that? "No," I said, "I've been nowhere near Chicago."

He pointed to a piece of steel that had been stamped with the words "Inland Steel," a well-known Chicago steel mill. We checked out several other pieces and all of them were stamped "Inland Steel." It made no sense.

I called Ed Murray at Republic and announced, "This steel you just sold me is not yours. It belongs to Inland; it has Inland stamps on it."

Ed was completely puzzled; he had no explanation.

"Someone at GM must have made a mistake and called you guys at Republic about the rejected steel instead of Inland," I said.

"OK," Ed said. "I'll take care of this."

A little while later, someone from Inland called me and told me that I could buy the steel for the same price I'd agreed upon with Republic; just send the check to them, not Republic. Republic, in turn, realized that they should have verified that the steel belonged to them before selling it to us, so they agreed to pick up the freight bill from the GM plant to my warehouse, by way of apology.

After that, I insisted that my men inspect every single piece of steel that came in to the warehouse. And I had a stamp made with my own company's trade name, Uniserv. Any flat steel we sold from then on was stamped with our name to make sure there would be no confusion.

Through the years, I kept a very close eye on expenses and invested my profits back into the company, and before long we were doing quite well. So well, in fact, that other companies began to ask about purchasing us.

Selling the company didn't seem like a bad idea to me; it might be nice to retire. For one thing, I could play golf every day. I could see Phyllis and myself moving to Florida and living by a beautiful golf course like Doral. I'd never heard of golf back in Czechoslovakia, but once I started playing it, I was hooked for life. Not only was it fun and a good way to socialize with people in business, it was a great way to take the measure of a man. On the links you can see how a person reacts to stress and how he behaves when he is about to lose the money he's bet on a game. Does he become rude, snide, or cantankerous? Pouty? Does he "create a convenient score"? You can also see how he handles victory, whether he is gracious and modest or tries to rub your nose in it. I got to know a lot of people very well by playing golf with them.

I'd had the privilege of playing golf on some really wonderful courses. But for years my big dream was to play at the famous course in Augusta, Georgia, a very exclusive private club. You could only play there if you were a member or the guest of a member, and becoming a member was very difficult. One day, I was playing at a local course with Paul Wilhelm, the president of U.S. Steel. When I mentioned that I would love to play at Augusta before I expired, Paul said casually, "Maybe I can make that happen."

I didn't think anything more about it until a few months later when Paul called and told me he'd arranged for me to play at Augusta! It was a dream come true to play as part of a foursome at this famous course with Paul, as well as Thomas Usher, the chairman of the board of U.S. Steel, and Jeffrey Bayman, who worked for me.

One time, I actually had the honor of playing with the great Arnold Palmer at Squaw Creek Country Club. He had just competed playing the U.S. Open at Oakmont Country Club, his last major tournament before retiring, and we were on the fifth hole when someone said to him, "I'll bet it's tough to play your last open."

The great golfer looked so upset at the remark, I felt sorry for him and said, "Mr. Palmer ..."

"Call me Arnie," he insisted.

"Thank you. Arnie, your best days are yet to come."

That made him smile. Maybe he thought I was just being nice, but I really believed what I said. Although we had only played five holes and chatted just a little, I could see he was a smart, gracious man—and, of course, a great athlete with the determination to push his way to the top. A man like Arnold Palmer doesn't just fade away. And I was right; he became a highly successful business executive, advertising spokesman, golf course designer, and consultant. Even more importantly, he became a major philanthropist, founding the Arnold Palmer Hospital for Children and the Arnold Palmer Prostate Center, among other charitable organizations.

But back to my dreams of retirement in 1974. Besides the appealing prospect of playing golf every day, there was another reason I was willing to consider selling. I had built my company to the point where were it was quite profitable, but to grow larger would be difficult without a very large infusion of cash. And even though I had excellent financials, the banks would only give me a certain amount of credit—not enough to make the leap to the next level. To get to that point would have taken years of frugal management and slow-but-steady growth. Maybe it was time to cash out and play golf.

One night, I was dining with my accountant, George Papp, at The Living Room, one of the best restaurants in Warren. While we were having drinks, I said to George, "If someone wanted to buy the business, how much should I ask for?"

Ever the accountant, George took a pen out of his pocket, tested it on a cocktail napkin and said, "Let's kick it around."

He asked me a lot of questions about the business, taking notes all the while, then made some calculations. Finally, he wrote a figure on the napkin and handed it to me, saying, "This is your price. Walk away if you don't get this figure."

Soon after that, I got a call from Ted Gaty, a friend and business associate, who said that a man named Grover Herman was interested in seeing my operation. Mr. Herman, Ted explained, was a substantial fellow, the former chairman of a large aerospace and electronics conglomerate called Martin Marietta, and the current owner of a conglomerate called Groman Corp. Could Ted show him the plant?

"Sure," I said. "Bring him by on Friday." And I told Ted my selling price, right then and there.

Friday morning, Ted was waiting for me by the front door with Grover Herman, a well-dressed man about seventy years old who was wearing a beautiful fur-collared coat. After we shook hands, I went back to my office while one of my assistants walked

Ted and Mr. Herman through the plant. About an hour later, they came to my office to chat. Mr. Herman also observed me on the telephone, buying and selling.

That evening, I met with Ted and he told me that Mr. Herman was interested in buying United Steel Service, but for a slightly lower price.

"No," I replied. "It's either full price or no sale."

I went home for the weekend and forgot all about Mr. Herman. Then Ted called again on Monday morning and told me that Mr. Herman would meet my price.

"Sold!" I said instantly. And that was that!

I had created, built, run, and sold a big steel business, more than fulfilling my boyhood dreams. But retirement was not in the cards, at least not right away, because as part of the deal I agreed to stay on and help run the company for another five years. I also retained ownership of the land and building, so I was now a rent-collecting landlord.

Running the company as part of a larger conglomerate had some advantages. For one thing, I could operate at a higher financial level and buy much larger quantities of steel. If I needed money, I simply called Groman Corp. headquarters in Chicago and told them how much I needed. Since I made a lot of money for them on my very first deal, they were always happy to supply me with money. And I, in turn, was happy to make bigger deals than I ever had in my life. It wasn't long before United Steel Service became one of their most profitable subsidiaries, and I was given a seat on the Groman Corp. board of directors. And a thought occurred to me: perhaps I could run Groman one day.

My relationship with Mr. Herman, I'm happy to say, was wonderful. He insisted early on that I call him by his first name. "To you, Morrie," he said, "it's Grover, not Mr. Herman." We spoke on the phone regularly, and once a month, he flew Phyllis and me out to Monterey, California to visit with him. His house was on the beautiful 17-Mile Drive, one of the most scenic drives in the world, which skirts the coast of the Pacific Ocean and runs right by the famous Pebble Beach Golf Links. Although Grover didn't golf, he arranged for me to play at different courses along the 17-Mile Drive. He was a very lovely man.

Things went along very well for several years until Grover passed away in 1980. Since he had not designated and prepared a successor, everything was up in the air while the company attorneys tried to sort things out. I immediately offered to run Groman Corp. and considered myself the logical choice. After all, I had been heading their most profitable subsidiary for years, and since I was also on the board of directors, I understood how the conglomerate operated. Plus, I had excellent contacts in the steel industry. The attorneys liked my idea, so I began talking to the heads of a few very large steel mills, suggesting that they take seats on the Groman board of directors once I took over.

"We could do a lot of business together," I said, and they agreed, realizing they could sell a lot of steel to the many companies in the Groman conglomerate.

Then they offered me an idea of their own.

"Have you ever thought about buying Groman? Why don't you run it for a while and, if things are looking good, we can help you buy it."

Now *that* was an interesting idea!

I pushed ahead, arranging with the attorneys to take over Mr. Herman's position as head of Groman Corp. without mentioning the idea of buying the company at some point. I kept that one under my hat. We forged ahead, and everything was looking good. But just as we were ready to conclude the deal, the head attorney told me that the deal was off. He didn't explain why; he just said that United Steel Service was "not in their scheme" and they were planning to sell the company. This, of course, meant that I would *not* be running Groman Corp. Once again, I was so close!

A few weeks later, the president of Groman Corp. brought some men to our plant who looked around and decided to buy United Steel Service from Groman. I still owned the land and the building, and collected a nice rent payment every month. Groman assured me that I would be well taken care of: the buyers were going to double my monthly rent payment and take a twenty- to thirty-year lease. At that point, it would have been very easy to do nothing and just collect a nice rent payment every month. But the idea of having my company sold out from under me stuck in my craw.

"No," I said. "I won't give them a lease."

The Groman president was surprised. He said, with sudden understanding, "You want to buy the company back!"

He was right. The Groman bigwigs were astonished, but there was really nothing they could do. Their lease on the land and the building was due to expire in just a couple of months. And since I refused to renew their lease, Groman would have to spend millions of dollars pulling their very heavy equipment out of my warehouse and setting it up in a different facility. On top of that, they knew there was nothing to stop me from opening a brand-new steel business in my warehouse—and if I did this, a lot of my customers would follow me. Groman would own my company's name and reputation, plus some equipment, but that was it.

All of these factors put me in a strong position to negotiate with Groman Corp. for the buyback, although it still cost me a great deal of money. I had to take a very hefty loan from the bank and sign the note personally, risking all of my personal assets, including my house and my savings, in order to get the loan. And down the line, if there was any trouble with the business and I couldn't make the loan payments, I could easily go bust.

My lawyer, Jay Skolnick, cautioned me about signing the note personally. "You'll never get off that note," he said. And my accountants and everyone else I spoke with agreed with him. Even if my company did well, they all said, the bank wouldn't want to take my name off the note. Why should they? My personal assets were just extra security for them; there would be no reason for them to let me off the hook.

But I pushed through the negotiations anyway, signed the note personally and took back my company. I even paid more than I needed to because I wanted the deal done, right now. My lawyer correctly pointed out that I had Groman over a barrel, but I didn't care. I wanted my company back.

"Finish the deal," I told Jay, "and get them out of here."

My very first decision as the new owner was that I *was* going to get my name off that note, come hell or high water. To do so, I would have to make the company as financially strong as possible. So I spent hours on the phone every day, buying and selling. I pored over all the invoices and other paperwork, constantly walked through the plant to see how the machines were running, and listened to what the workers had to say about everything.

And, always keeping an eye on the books, I waited for the day when United Steel Service would be financially sound enough so I could get off that note. I kept a close eye on operations, and several years after the buyback, the company had grown financially. One day I asked our treasurer, Joel Miller, where we stood, and he told me that our asset-to-liabilities ratio was 3:1. In other words, for every $3 in assets, we had only $1 in liabilities, an excellent ratio for a company in our business.

Carl Summers, the Treasurer at Youngstown Sheet and Tube, really understood finances and knew I was trying to get off the note. When he asked me to show him my company's financial statement, I laid the papers on his desk and he looked through them carefully. Then he looked up at me and said, "Morris, this is good. You'll be able to find a bank to take you off the note."

At long last, it was time. But instead of going back to the bank that had given me the original loan, Union Savings and Trust, I went to another bank, where I sat with the president, explained my financial situation, and asked if they would lend enough money to my company that I could pay off my personal guarantee and get off the note. He seemed surprised, and replied, "I don't know why you came all the way out here. With these figures, any bank will give you the loan."

Once I had this backup arranged, I went to see Chuck Foley at the bank where my original loan was held. In a friendly manner, I pointed out my company's asset-to-liability ratio and said, "Chuck, I want you to take me off the note. Today. By noon."

He looked surprised and asked, "Where are you going?" He probably guessed I had lined up a backup bank. I just repeated, "I want to be off the note. By noon."

"Well, let me see what the man upstairs says."

Chuck called the president of the bank, told him what I wanted, and hung up. A minute later the bank president came into Chuck's office and, without looking at me, said to Chuck, "Get him off the note."

I received written confirmation by noon. United Steel Service belonged to me again, lock, stock, and barrel. And I was off the note!

To this day, at the ripe old age of ninety-five, I continue to own United Steel Service, although my son, Steven, is now CEO. I serve as Chairman of the Board and go in to work several days a week, mostly to look things over. I'm still convinced that checking everything carefully is very important. Although it's tempting for the Chairman of the Board, the CEO, or even middle managers to stay locked up in their offices and spend their days going to

meetings and shuffling papers, if you do so, the business will suffer. Every day, you need to go to the plant, workshop, cubicles, or
wherever else the work is done to keep tabs on what's going on.

It is also very important to take good care of your employees. Everything is computerized and high-tech these days, so it's
easy to think that people don't matter much anymore. But that's
wrong. Your people *are* your business. They can go the extra mile
to make sure the job is done exactly right, or just do the minimum
to get by. My advice is to hire good people, compensate them well,
treat them fairly, and make it clear that you expect the best from
them. Then personally get to know as many of them as you can.
Call them by name, greet them whenever you see them, and ask
them how things are going. Your employees know things that you
don't know about your business, and they can spot trouble before
it happens. Ask for their ideas and listen to their complaints. Then
take action, when it seems warranted. If you treat your employees
this way, nine times out of ten they'll give you their best, and more.

I'm also a big believer in going the extra mile for my employees, not only for their benefit but also for my own peace of mind.
For example, we've always had a nice health insurance plan for our
employees, but sometimes it's just not enough. One of our employees, a fellow named Jim, worked in our warehouse sharpening our
slitter knives. When he developed a rare and fatal form of cancer,
his doctors wanted to treat him with experimental bone marrow
transplants. But the insurance company refused to cover the cost,
and since there was no other treatment, Jim was told he didn't
have much longer to live. This seemed ridiculous to me: Jim was
going to die because the insurance company didn't want to pay? I

found out that the bone marrow transplants were being conducted at the University of Nebraska and told Jim that all would be taken care of. You can imagine my joy when Jim's treatments were successful and he recovered! I was thrilled to have had the chance to give Jim a new lease on life, and he continued to keep our slitter knives razor-sharp for another twenty years.

There is another rule I have always followed, which is to buy American. American steel companies produced much of the world's quality steel for a good twenty years after World War II. But in the 1970s and 1980s, other countries began to offer serious competition. I could easily have made more money if I'd started buying foreign steel, but I never did, because I love this country. I have always wanted to give something back to this wonderful country, and one way I can do it is by helping to keep the steel industry strong. I certainly can't revive the entire industry by myself, of course: the amount of steel I've purchased over the years is just a tiny drop in a much larger bucket. But I'll always do my part by buying American to keep Americans working.

United Steel Service has been in operation for over forty years, growing during the good times and managing to hold on through the bad times. For decades, our business served as a middleman between the mills and smaller customers, buying prime overruns or irregulars and reselling them, as well as slitting the steel for certain customers. Long-standing relationships, warmed by a friendly chat over a nice lunch with brandy and cigars, often led to a lot of business. But that's not allowed anymore: today, there are rules that prevent you from getting close to the people at the mills. Also, since computers control steel production, there are far fewer overruns or batches of irregular steel. For these and other reasons, I closed down the warehouse part of our operation in 2011, and we no longer wheel and deal.

Instead, we focus on skill and precision. Today, United Steel Service is strictly a slitting operation, cutting steel coils into the smaller sizes requested by our customers. The customers purchase the coils and ship them to us; we slit them and ship them out. We're a specialty operation with machinery and expertise that can't be found in many other places.

In the forty-plus years that have passed since I sat on an orange crate in a borrowed office, United Steel Service has employed as many as 200 men and women at a time in our warehouse, plant, and offices. We've bought and sold thousands of tons of steel from all over the country, and slit thousands of tons. I've made some good decisions and some bad ones—we set up a branch in Florida in the 1980s that didn't work out, and we took a bath on it. But that's the business.

I'm immensely proud of my company, our employees, our work, and the steel business itself. Every time I walk through our plant, I feel like a boy again, ready to conquer the world. And I'm doing it in the country I love, with my son at my side.

It's been a wonderful life. And it could only have happened in America.

Three men who greatly influenced Morrie's career: from left to right,
Dudley Jones, Jacob "Uncle Jack" Friedman, Herman "Uncle Herman" Friedman.

Arnold Palmer looks on as Morrie takes a shot.

Morrie and Arnold Palmer share a moment.

Dear Nephew Morris:

Some of our relatives have said that you were making commissions from Allieds operations. I know of the facts in connection with all of these deals and they have been done with my full knowledge and consent.

Anyone who has been in the steel business as long as I have knows the facts of life/what and sometimes must be done to satisfy everyone and still keep the big end of the profit. I do appreciate what you have been able to do for Allied in the various matters. Any extra commissions which you received were meant to be in addition to your salary and represented many hours of extra work by you. After all, Allied received the big share of the benefit. As we both know, no part of your commission were shared with me. My only interest was the success of Allied Metals Co.

[signature: Jacob Friedman]

A letter from Jacob "Uncle Jack" Friedman clearly illustrating his business relationship with Morrie.

Memo FROM: J. Friedman

TO:

L. E. Moore
The Allied Metals Company
Niles, Ohio

DATE: February 22, 1965

SUBJECT: Morris Friedman
————FOLD HERE———— xΩxxxxkxxkxxxxxxn Slitting Line - Warren Plant

Effective February 1, 1965, added Compensation shall be
paid to Morris Friedman of fifty cents ($0.50) per net
ton on all tonnage slit on the 66" Paxson Slitter located
at the Warren Plant of The Allied Metals Company.
This will be effective until further notice.

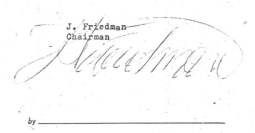

J. Friedman
Chairman

by _____

A memo to the Treasurer of Allied Metals clearly illustrating
Jacob "Uncle Jack" Friedman's wishes for Morrie's compensation.

Service
with
Sincerity

UNISERV

UNITED STEEL SERVICE, INC.

United Steel Service, Incorporated, the company Morrie built.

PART II:

MY PHILOSOPHY

CHAPTER TEN

The Dream of America

I'm ninety-five years old, so I've been around for a long time. Long enough to remember an America that was the envy of the world. But now I'm heartbroken to say that the America I knew is on the verge of vanishing completely.

I'm talking about an America that was openly proud of its history, flag and Constitution. An America that ...

...firmly believed in liberty and democracy.

...encouraged and embraced the capitalism that improved the lives of every citizen.

...was brave enough to say that democratic capitalism linked to Judeo-Christian values is the best system in the world.

...was willing to go toe-to-toe with the Nazis, the Communists, and anyone else who threatened to destroy us.

...had the military might to take over much of the world but did not, because it was decent, honorable, and generous.

...valued a hard day's work and believed that taking a handout was embarrassing.

...respected the industrialists who provided jobs that enriched us all.

...valued the teachers who prepared the next generation to succeed.

...believed that the future was unlimited and embraced impossible ideas like completely rebuilding war-torn Europe and sending a man to the moon.

...was filled with men and women, including me, who were literally willing to die for this country and what it stood for.

It was an America that I loved dearly and that, unfortunately, is fading away. Or maybe I should say it is being thrown away, because that's what our politicians and other "leaders" have been doing for decades. They are throwing America away with both hands, contemptuously spitting on it and grinding it into the dust with their heels. And this hurts me very much because the America I knew and treasured was, as Abraham Lincoln said, "the last, best hope of earth."

I was born and raised in a country that lacked even a shred of the decency and opportunity found in America. It was a place where the government deliberately set one group against another; where citizens had to yield the sidewalk to government officials, even if it meant stepping into muck or manure; where your future was limited simply because you were born into one group and not another; where people would laugh at you for dreaming of a better life.

I was lucky enough to get out of Czechoslovakia before it was destroyed by the Nazis, and sailed to the United States in the bottom of a ship, all alone, when I was just fifteen years old. I left so fast I didn't even have time to say goodbye to my mother, who was murdered by the Nazis with my father and two younger brothers, along with millions of Jews, gypsies, homosexuals, and other people considered undesirable.

I can't tell you how lucky I was to make it to the United States, and words cannot convey how much I love this country. It's impossible to describe the feelings that washed over me, a desperately poor and lonely little Jew, one of the most despised members of my Old World society, as I watched the Statue of Liberty grow larger and larger when we finally sailed into New York harbor. Even then, before I had learned a word of English, when I had only seen a few cowboy movies and some pictures from American magazines, I knew what that beautiful statue meant—it meant my life was starting over. And this time, I would have a chance to make something of myself.

Since arriving in the United States nearly eighty years ago, I've had many chances to make something of myself and seen many of my dreams come true: I became an American citizen; I fought for democracy in World War II; I made money in the steel industry; and I've been treated very well by people of all colors and religions. I also married the woman of my dreams, and we had a wonderful son together. At this point in my life, I should be very satisfied, and I am. But I'm also worried, because over the past several decades I've watched everything America stands for mocked, if not destroyed.

Today, our children grow up believing that ...

...this country is evil.

...we are no better (and may be worse) than the terrorists and others who want to destroy us.

...working hard to achieve something is not as important as simply feeling good about yourself.

...surviving on government handouts is perfectly acceptable, even if you're quite capable of working.

...speaking truthfully and from the heart is harmful, and every word you utter must always be "politically correct."

...immigrants don't need to enter this country legally or even want to become Americans. And it's okay if they refuse to learn the language, study our history, or absorb our values.

...and, perhaps worst of all, that no one can succeed without the help and guidance of a powerful, intrusive government.

Pardon me for saying so, but this is all a load of crap.

Yes, there are some things wrong with America. We have made many mistakes and are still struggling with the fallout from past errors, such as racial bigotry and misguided economic policies. But just think what this world would be like today if our country had *not* been willing to stand up for its values, if the Nazis or Communists or radical Islamists had been allowed to take over, or if we had *not* spread democracy and capitalism and the freedom and prosperity they bring throughout the world.

And imagine what will happen to the world if America continues to doubt itself, and because of that doubt to weaken, to lose its will and strength—which will happen, unless we turn our backs on the politicians and "advanced thinkers" who have sown and watered the seeds of doubt in our citizens. So many of us doubt that we are good, that we are able to take care of ourselves, that our philosophies are good and have merit, that the most basic things our country stands for are worthwhile. Instead, so many of our political leaders and activists tell us we should put all of our efforts into simply being loved by other countries and keeping the peace at all costs.

These are incredibly destructive ideas, but they have taken firm hold in our society over the past several decades. That's why I worry. And that's why I wrote this book. I want to tell people what America meant to the world so many years ago. And I want to explain what we, its citizens, need to do to help our country find itself again, so it can lead the world to a better, freer, more prosperous future for all people.

I'm not a politician or a professor; I don't even have a college degree. I haven't visited fifty-seven different countries or studied the constitutions of sixty-two others. I'm just a guy who has worked in the steel industry for over seventy-five years, as a messenger, a factory hand, a manager, a buyer, an executive, and the owner of my own company. I'm a regular guy who has had to worry about things like paying the rent, keeping my workers employed, raising my family, and having something left over to donate to charity.

But because I've lived in the real world for a very long time and know what it's like, I'm in a good position to understand and sum up what's been happening to our country over the past many decades. Career politicians, professors, community organizers, and others who are leading this country may know a lot of things, but few of them have ever had to run a business or worry about making the weekly payroll. They spend their lives in a bubble, where all kinds of crazy ideas seem to make sense. It may even seem "smart" to denigrate and destroy values and beliefs that form the foundation of our country and make the world a better place.

Enough of that already! I'm on a mission to remind our citizens, especially the young ones who have grown up in a self-hating America, of our sacred values and their importance to us as individuals and a nation, and to the world. And why we must resurrect the values that made our country great and learn to love America once again.

The Dream of America

To me, America is a dream. Imagine you're a poor child living in poverty, like I was, in some other country. The kind of poverty I'm talking about is worse than not having enough food to fill your belly or clothes to keep you warm. It's a poverty of possibilities: for you, there are none. You are born into a certain position in life that defines you and boxes you in. Because of your religion, dialect, address, skin color, caste, or some other attribute, your life is pretty much predetermined. When I was born in Czechoslovakia almost one hundred years ago, I was automatically labeled "poor" and "farm boy" and a few other things that meant I would probably never rise above being a baker or shopkeeper. My box was also labeled "Jew," which meant I was, by definition, a lesser being. (And believe me, the anti-Semitism I personally faced was nothing compared to what happened shortly after I fled Europe and the Nazis began their slaughter.)

When you are stuffed into a little box labeled "Jew" or "untouchable," or whatever the negative label may be in your society, your possibilities are limited and mostly unpleasant. You cannot hope for a better future. You just hope to get enough food to eat today, or to have a few pennies left over at the end of the week, or to avoid being kicked by one of your "betters." Or maybe you hope for darker things, like taking revenge on the society or people who keep you down. When you do dream the big dream of the future, when you dream of being in a place where impossibly wonderful things come true, you dream of America.

Those who were born and raised in America can never fully realize what it means to those living in downtrodden areas who long for a better life. Millions of people with great dreams have left their homelands, their families, and everything they've ever known to come here. They have had all kinds of dreams: To be free to practice their religion. To make a better life for their children. To go into business and get rich. Or they want to get away from the misery in their home countries. I'm not saying every dream comes true in this country, that everyone becomes rich or that it is easy to do so. Many people struggle to stay afloat, and many others make it only part way up the ladder before they fall back down again. Often, the first generation toils away in low-level jobs to ensure that the second generation will have the chance to be educated and find good jobs. While not every dream comes true, there are endless possibilities in America, a place where dreams *can* come true. Just think of Abraham Lincoln and our current president, Barack Obama, who both went from nowhere all the way to the top.

Exploring the Dream

So what is it that makes America so special? There are many very nice countries like England and Sweden and Japan that are modern and prosperous and run on democratic and capitalistic principles. Why don't people around the world dream about escaping to these countries? Some do, but many more come to America. Why? I believe the reason America is "the land where dreams come true" can be found in our Declaration of Independence, in the lines that say:

We hold these truths to be self-evident, that all men are created equal, that they are endowed by their Creator with certain unalienable Rights, that among these are Life, Liberty and the pursuit of Happiness.

These thirty-five words tell us that in this country there are no borders drawn around you before you are born, no distinctions of religion or caste or color or anything else to hold you back, as long as you're willing to push ahead. Our founding fathers set the tone for our nation by clearly stating that there is a universal Creator, that he has granted us certain rights, and that these rights are *not* subject to change and *cannot* be revoked. These rights include "Life, Liberty and the pursuit of Happiness."

The first of these three items, "life," is very straightforward: the government cannot wage war on its own people. The second, "liberty," includes the rights to practice the religion of your choice, to speak your mind even if what you say offends others, to challenge government and its actions, to be considered innocent until proven guilty, and much more. As for the "pursuit of happiness," our founding fathers understood that it is impossible to ensure happiness or to pass laws guaranteed to make our citizens happy. So they used the wording "pursuit of happiness." You are guaranteed the right to strive, to dream of what might be, and to work to achieve it.

All that has made America the greatest nation on earth flows from these simple ideas.

I didn't know anything about these words or the Declaration of Independence when I was a boy in Vapenik. But I knew my uncles in America had started a business and become wealthy, despite being poorly educated foreigners without money or connections. And even though they were Jewish, they were safe in America, which was not the case in Europe. So I knew that if I went to America, I would also be safe. And I would have a chance to make my own life. Back then, I couldn't image a better dream than that, and I still feel the same way today.

America is not just a dream—it's a dream come true for millions and millions and millions of people.

CHAPTER ELEVEN

A Strong America, A Better World

Even though the country was in the midst of the Great Depression when I arrived in 1936, people everywhere were dreaming of a better future. Of course, some were really down and out and could not see their way to a better life, but almost all of the people I met in New York, Cleveland, and Niles were talking about tomorrow and how good it was going to be. These weren't big business owners or wealthy people; they were just regular folks: storekeepers, factory workers, and clerks. As for me, I already thought life was wonderful. In the Bronx, my relatives ran just a little neighborhood grocery store, but even *they* had enough money to live like kings—at least in my mind.

Today, however, the idea of a wonderful future has all but died out. Few Americans seem to believe that our country continues to be the land where dreams come true. And few believe that America has done much to make the world a better place and continues to do so. Instead, we are told by some of our leaders, professors, authors, and journalists that this country has done terrible things, for we are a fundamentally evil nation. They say:

- We use our financial power to overpower smaller nations so we can siphon off their resources.

- We take advantage of laborers in poor countries so we can buy things more cheaply.

- We wage war on one nation after another for our own selfish purposes.

- We manipulate our economy and our laws to keep millions of our own citizens trapped in poverty.

- We are so riddled with racism and bigotry that we can never change.

And these are just a few of the accusations!

Are We Evil?

These are serious charges, but are they true? Instead of taking each one by itself, let's look at the major theme, that America is fundamentally evil. Is there any proof that this is at all true? Well, we have done many things wrong, there's no doubt about that. Slavery is a good example. And even after slavery was abolished, Jim Crow laws continued to prevent blacks from being fully protected by the law, while restricting their efforts to educate and advance themselves.

On the other hand, there were many citizens who were against slavery right from the start, and as we all know, our nation went to war with itself to eliminate it. And many people fought for the passage of the 1960s Civil Rights bills, reinforcing the idea that *everyone* has the right to life, liberty, and the pursuit of happiness. It took us a long time to undo our wrongdoing, but if we were really an evil nation, would we have even tried?

If we were so terrible, we would have done things a lot differently. For example, we could have:

- Let the Germans crush France during World War I, or allowed Germany to conquer all of Europe during World War II. In both wars, the United States was separated from the battlefields by the big, wide Atlantic Ocean. What was happening in Europe really wasn't our problem, so we could have easily have sat on our hands, waited for the dust to settle, then profited by trading with the victor. Instead, we sent our American boys to fight and die for freedom in Europe.

- Completely wiped out Japan following World War II and done the same things to them they did to other countries (mass murder, torture, starvation). Instead, we re-created the Japanese government as a democracy, and allowed Japan to become a free and prosperous country.

- Made a deal with the Soviet Union during the long decades of the Cold War. Rather than standing up to Communism over and over again, we could have said, "We'll control this half of the world, and you can control the other half." Instead, we fought for liberty and democracy all over the world for decades, at great cost, until the Soviet Union finally collapsed.

- Cut way back on legal immigration and let in only a few foreigners who had the exact job skills we needed, and then kicked them out when we were done with them. Instead, there are now around 40 million immigrants living in the United States, and even though our country accounts for less than five percent of the world's population, we take in 20 percent of the world's immigrants!

- Rounded up the nearly 12 million illegal immigrants currently residing in our country, expelled them, or put them in work camps and profited from their labor. Instead, we allow the overwhelming majority of them to live and work among us, enjoying many of the same protections and benefits as we citizens do. Just recently, President Obama ordered the Immigration and Customs Enforcement agency to simply ignore the vast majority of our illegal immigrants and focus on the ones who had committed crimes since they had come to our country.

- Walked away from the United Nations and other international governing bodies by now. After all, these organizations often vote against the U.S., or have been taken over by our enemies, who use them as clubs to beat us over the head. Instead, we are the largest single contributor to the United Nations and affiliated organizations.

- Abolished Social Security, Medicare, and the many other programs that provide aid to the needy. Instead, our federal government spends well over $600 billion a year on welfare and related programs. The state and local governments also contribute a great deal to their own programs, while individuals, corporations, and foundations donate an additional $300 billion-plus annually. While people on both sides of the political spectrum argue about how much money we should provide to the needy and how the various programs should be structured, no one suggests we cut off all aid. We are a very generous nation.

- Hung on to the incredible new discoveries and inventions emanating from our universities and corporations, so that only we could profit from them. Instead, we share the fruits of our research at international conferences and in journals, allowing other countries and their companies to use the knowledge we have generated to become more prosperous.

I could list many more examples, but the point is clear: We are *not* an evil nation. We have made mistakes in the past and will make more in the future, but we are fundamentally a good and generous country.

A Strong America Equals a Better World

The world has become a better place in so many ways since America rose to the top. Although I could list many, let's look at three of the most important. First, America keeps the world free; second, America fosters creativity; and third, the American system generates world-wide wealth.

America Keeps the World Free

Most of us take democracy for granted because it works so well and we're used to it. In fact, many of us don't even bother to vote because we feel so confident that democracy will always be around and we don't need to make the slightest effort to participate in it, let alone protect it.

But democracy is a fragile concept. During our country's first hundred years, only a handful of other countries became democratic. By 1900, there were about twelve, an incredible number for the time. It looked like democracy would spread across the world, but as Europe exploded into World War I and the Great Depression ruined economies around the world, democracy was in trouble. Communism, fascism, and military dictatorships replaced democracies in one country after another. As we approached World War II, many wondered if democracy would be able to survive.

Even after World War II ended, the situation was not rosy for democracy. The Soviet Union did the opposite to the Eastern European countries, forcing them to become Communist. The Communists took over China in 1949, and their corrupt philosophy spread throughout Southeast Asia, Africa, the Middle East, and Central and South America in the decades that followed. And even in democratic Western Europe, Communist parties grew strong and gained a measure of power.

If we were selfish or lazy, we could have just kept to ourselves and ignored the rest of the world. We could have built strong defenses for the United States, created alliances with England, Canada, and other like-minded countries, and turned our backs on the rest of the world. We didn't need anybody else at the time: we were rich, and we had a strong manufacturing base and a tremendous amount of natural resources—we were even exporting oil back then! It wouldn't have hurt us a bit to let one country after another be swallowed up by the Communists, or turned into yet another brutal military or religious dictatorship.

But we didn't. We believed that we had a duty to spread freedom and the democratic form of government that protects it. And we felt obligated to spill our blood in order to help oppressed people.

Democracy doesn't just happen. It's not a natural state that just arises without effort; it takes hard work to create it. It's despised by autocrats, dictators, Communists, and others who want to grab all the power and oppress their people. Democracy, then, has to be won and protected, and the fight can be difficult.

By 1974, only thirty countries worldwide could be called democracies. Because America continued to support democracy financially and militarily, and showed the world by example how much better life could be in a free and capitalist country, over 100 countries are democracies today. Never before has the world been as free and democratic as it is now.

This is *not* an accident, and it didn't happen because of demographics or some other forces of history. Democracy is strong today *because and only because* the United States is and has been the dominant power. Think about the misery inflicted by Communism and military/religious dictatorships on hundreds of millions of people around the world. Think about the tens of millions of people slaughtered or deliberately starved *by their own governments* in Russia, China, North Korea, Cambodia, and so many other countries. Think about what happens when radical religious regimes take control, literally chopping off the heads of those who dare to oppose them.

America is the fountainhead of democracy, and the freedom and prosperity it brings. Democracy has flourished under our protective umbrella.

America Fosters Creativity

I just finished reading an article in the *Wall Street Journal* about the countries that have won the most Nobel prizes and the reasons why. This article points out that since the year 2000, "Americans have won 21 of the 37 physics prizes, 18 of the 33 medicine prizes, 22 of the 33 chemistry prizes, and an astonishing 27 of the 30 economic prizes." If you look at ten countries that have won the most Nobels since the prize was first awarded in 1901, you'll see something even more amazing: the United States has won 347, compared to 120 for Great Britain, 104 for Germany, 65 for France, 30 for Sweden, 27 for Russia, 26 for Switzerland, 23 for Canada, 22 for Austria, and 20 for Italy.

You might say that the U.S. wins so many Nobel prizes just because we have a large population. But Russia also has a large population, and the populations of China and India dwarf ours. You might also say that the U.S. has an advantage because it is wealthy—but so are many other countries on the list.

The main reason we have won the lion's share of Nobel prizes is that we are a magnet for smart and creative people from all over the world. Our system rewards those who come up with new ideas, who study hard, think outside of the box, and take chances. Our universities and private research laboratories are chock full of highly intelligent and creative people. And the federal government, entrepreneurs, and many corporations are willing to pay people large salaries just to be creative. It's not surprising that the U.S. has long attracted imaginative people from all over the world who come here to study and work. Other countries do not reward creativity the way we do. Just think about how creative you would be if you were working in a Soviet gulag with a gun to your head (figuratively), or slaving away in a country whose laws made it difficult for you to profit from your own ideas.

There are other ways to measure a nation's creativity: you can look at the sheer number and variety of ideas, inventions, and techniques coming out of any given country. Here, too, the U.S. shines. Some of the many ideas, creations or techniques that originated in America include adhesive bandages, air bags, air conditioning, assembly lines, automatic transmissions, barcodes, bifocals, blogging, Broadway musicals, cash registers, chewing gum, Coca-Cola, compact discs, cruise control, dental floss, digital cameras, dishwashers, disposable diapers, electric fans, email, escalators, Facebook, Ferris wheels, fire hydrants, flashlights, fortune cookies, GPS (global positioning system), the Heimlich maneuver, the Internet, jackhammers, jeans, Kevlar, lasers, laser printers, leaf blowers, light bulbs, lightning rods, mail order, microwave ovens, mobile phones, Morse code, mousetraps, MRI (magnetic resonance imaging), nylon, paper towels, personal computers, potato chips, refrigeration, remote controls, revolvers, supermarkets, swivel chairs, tea bags, Teddy bears, Teflon, vacuum cleaners, video tape, windshield wipers, wrenches, YouTube, and zippers. We were even able to send men to the moon! And this is just a (very) short list.

The American System Generates Worldwide Wealth

National wealth doesn't increase on its own; conditions have to be created to encourage its growth. And for much of history, the world's wealth didn't grow much at all. If you look at the world's collective gross domestic product (GDP), you'll see that it increased by an average of less than 1 percent per year between 1550 and 1950. But since 1950, when the U.S. became the dominant country, the GDP has risen by about 4 percent annually. That's quite a difference!

There are several reasons for this, including the fact that there have been no major-power wars in the nearly seventy years since World War II ended. For centuries before World War II, there were endless wars between England, Russia, France, Prussia, and other major powers. These countries poured money into their armies and navies, interrupted trade, destroyed fertile land, and levied taxes to pay for their wars. It's true that war can enrich a few individual countries: we emerged from World War II in a very favorable financial position. Overall, however, major wars destroy wealth.

But since America became the world's mightiest nation and its "policeman," there have been no wars between the major powers. Just imagine the annihilation of wealth that would result from a war between the U.S. and Russia, or China and Russia, or any other combination of major powers. Billions of dollars would be chewed up to finance the war; millions of productive workers would be snatched away from their workplaces and put in uniform; millions of students would have their educations interrupted. And how many of these workers and students would perish, taking their skills and knowledge with them? Cities would be reduced to rubble, and productive land would be laid to waste or made uninhabitable by nuclear fallout.

A second reason the world's wealth has increased so dramatically since America took up the reins of power is that we are a capitalist country, and capitalism is much better at generating and spreading wealth than any other system. Just look at the obvious differences in wealth between capitalist United States and the Communist Soviet Union, beginning at the end of World War II and running through the Cold War. The U.S. was the leader of the free world and Russia was the chief Communist country. Both were roughly comparable in population and had abundant natural resources.

The GDP of the U.S. was $2.22 trillion in 1945, the year World War II ended; $4.10 trillion in 1965; $7.71 trillion in 1985; $14.37 trillion in 2005; and $15.99 trillion today, in 2014, as we continue to recover from the Great Recession. We've had our ups and downs, but the trend is clear: our national wealth has steadily increased. Suburbs, industrial parks, and universities have sprung up across the country; garages are filled with cars and RVs and "stuff"; average people take vacations across the country and even overseas; homes are loaded with computers, electronic devices, multiple TVs, and labor-saving devices. We still have poor people in this country, but their standard of living is much higher than that of the poor in most other countries.

Compare this to living conditions in the Soviet Union during that time, where people lived in ugly, dated concrete apartment buildings, did not own a single car, stood in long lines to buy food, and had to wait years to get something as simple as a new refrigerator. This miserable situation was not confined to Russia; the people in China, North Korea, and most every other Communist country suffered just as much, or even more.

There's no doubt that democratic capitalism is much better at generating wealth, mostly because it rewards people for their efforts. Today, China is becoming wealthy—but only because its leaders finally dropped Communist economic theory and slowly but surely introduced capitalism. It's not full capitalism yet, and certainly not democratic capitalism, but it is enough to supercharge their economy.

The Dream of America Is the World's Dream

Human beings are not perfect, so the world will never be ideal. But as long as a democratic, capitalist United States remains strong and is driven by a desire to spread life, liberty, and the pursuit of happiness, the world will continue to improve, become freer and wealthier, and better the lives of people across the globe.

Chapter Twelve

Regaining Our Powerful Vision

Although America has saved the world from misery many times and in many ways, we somehow seem unable to rescue ourselves from fear, doubt, and self-loathing.

I see this in so many people, especially young people fresh from the university, who tell me that America is bent on world domination, that our "white man culture" is hateful, boring, and destructive. These attitudes don't just show up out of nowhere. The seeds of self-doubt and self-hatred were planted in the minds of these students long ago, when they were very young.

Don't get me wrong: there is often good reason to doubt the wisdom of our leaders and believe that certain policies, laws, or wars are unwise. In fact, it's good to challenge our leaders and make them either justify their actions to our satisfaction or alter them. But there's a big difference between healthy debate and vigorous political action, on the one hand, and plain old self-hatred on the other.

Doubting our current leaders or their actions can spur us to action, but doubting ourselves can lead to disaster. And decade after decade of nothing but doubt is a recipe for national disaster. Just like a person who is depressed, our nation is feeling helpless, hopeless, guilty, and worthless; it lacks energy and has lost its focus. Unfortunately, there is no magic pill that can instantly erase our national depression. Instead, our salvation lies in remembering our founding principles—in remembering the dream of America.

More Pluses, Fewer Minuses

What we really need today in America is to emphasize the things that make this country great (the pluses) and de-emphasize the things that make us weaker (the minuses). I've already talked about our major pluses, which stem from those beautiful words in our Declaration of Independence: "We hold these truths to be self-evident, that all men are created equal, that they are endowed by their Creator with certain unalienable Rights, that among these are Life, Liberty and the pursuit of Happiness."

In other words:

- We are personally free, able to choose our paths in life without being boxed in by circumstances of birth.
- We enjoy religious freedom, worshiping the Creator as we choose—or not worshiping at all, for being an atheist is also our right.
- We are free to join the political party and vote for the candidate of our choice.
- We have the power to tell our leaders to take a hike by voting them out of office—and we should do so more often.
- We can always hold our heads high, no matter what our background or present circumstances.

- We can dare to dream any dream and climb as high up the ladder of success as our talent, drive, and good fortune will allow.

- We are free to fail, fail, and fail again, then start all over again before succeeding.

As for the minuses, here's a short list:

- We have forgotten that we stand for life, liberty, and the pursuit of happiness.

- We have forgotten that we are a united people belonging to a single nation. Instead, we are splintered into political, religious, ethnic, economic, and other factions, each of which believes that "the others" are hell-bent on ruining the country.

- We have forgotten that the world is a better place because of what America has done. Instead, we wring our hands every time we're criticized by a leader, newspaper, or group from some other country.

- We have turned against ourselves and our beliefs, our history, and our tremendous contributions to the world. Learned professors in universities across the country teach our young people that America is a selfish, greedy, warmonger; that our culture is bankrupt; and that our society is irredeemably prejudiced. And while they are preaching this lopsided view of America, they "forget" to mention all of the great things our country has accomplished.

- Our leaders are more focused on themselves than on the greater good. Our founding fathers pledged "our Lives, our Fortunes and our sacred Honor" to each other and to their great cause. Today, our leaders mostly worry about the effect their actions will have on next year's election results.

- We have replaced "government of the people, by the people, for the people" with a government run by career politicians, lobbyists, and special interest groups. Career politicians have one overriding need, which is to remain in office. Everything else is subordinate to that goal. As for lobbyists and special interest groups, in 2014 they lined the pockets of our national and state leaders with billions of dollars in donations. But they don't hand out that money for fun. They expect, and receive, special considerations in return.

- We have allowed the word "wealthy" to become a nasty word. In our capitalist system, the ability to accumulate wealth is the reward that spurs us to work hard and to keep trying when things are not going well. While some people become wealthy through accident of birth or crooked means, most wealthy Americans have worked hard to get where they are. They should be applauded, not scorned. More of us should follow their example.

- We have weakened our citizens by dispensing welfare and other forms of support without asking for anything back from those who are able. You don't have to be a professor to know that people respond to incentives. Giving generous benefits to those who are capable of working without requiring them to do something in return removes the incentive to get off welfare.

- We teach our children that feeling good about themselves is better than working to achieve something. A true feeling of pride comes from achieving something, from overcoming obstacles and helping others. Applauding people for doing nothing in a misguided attempt to build their self-esteem is nonsense—and a true negative for the country in general.

- We teach our children that it's wrong to say that this nation is good, because everything is relative and subjective. If that's true, why don't the people who believe this take their children and move to North Korea? Since everything is relative and subjective, they can have very nice lives there.

- We have let political correctness run amok. You should always be polite to others and think before you speak. But there is something seriously wrong when you can get into trouble for saying "Oriental" instead of "Asian," or "Negro" instead of "black." Instead of focusing on the meaning of what people say, we censor them when they use a word somebody has deemed offensive. This is a form of thought control and a way to shut down unpopular ideas. That's not what our founding fathers wanted when they created this country.

- We have lost our love for a goods day's work, forgotten the satisfaction that comes from sweating to succeed. It is now considered perfectly acceptable to live off the government.

- We look to Washington to solve all of our problems and tell us what to do. Too many of us look to Big Brother to solve our problems for us, rather than put in the sweat necessary to solve them on our own.

Nothing good ever came of denigrating, debasing, or running down a person, an enterprise, or a country. We desperately need to build up and protect our national storehouse of pluses and downplay the minuses if our country is to regain its health and stability.

New Beliefs, New Beginnings

You're probably thinking, "It's easy to say that we need to increase our pluses while reducing our minuses. But how, exactly, can we do that?" The one thing that all pluses and minuses have in common is they are based on beliefs, so that's where we should start—by changing our beliefs. The beliefs I think we need to reinstate into the national thinking, teach our children, and remind ourselves of every day include:

1. The United States is a wonderful country, with a rich history and culture and long list of accomplishments. We admire and respect other nations and peoples, but we love the U.S.A.!

2. Our Judeo-Christian heritage has been a positive guiding force. It must be nourished and cherished.

3. As long as the U.S. remains strong and involved in world affairs, the world will be an increasingly better place.

4. Some countries, cultures, and/or religions are *good*, while others are *bad*.

5. Our government should always and only work *for* the people.

6. We must give generously to those who are genuinely unable to care for themselves—but everyone else works.

7. When given a choice between smaller and larger government, we should always choose smaller and return the responsibility to the people.

Let's take a close look at these beliefs.

The United States Is a Wonderful Country

I come from a place where dukes, barons, and other nobles happily oppressed everyone beneath them for centuries—and just about everyone was far beneath them. The fact that the nobles grabbed all the wealth and power for themselves was not unusual; there have always been those who do this. What was truly terrible about them was that they considered themselves naturally and irrevocably superior to everyone else by virtue of their birth. They believed they had been selected by God to rule all the "lesser beings." Very few of these dukes and barons ever earned their positions; most inherited their power and wealth. Yet in their minds, everyone else was inferior, incapable of being "civilized" or acquiring knowledge and, for the most part, mentally feeble and morally corrupt.

In America, however, we believe that everyone is equal, and that is the foremost reason I am so proud of this country. Our founders dared to make this idea a major pillar of their new government. Too much time passed before this idea became reality, but citizens from across the country fought and died until it did.

If this were the only wonderful thing we could point to about our country, it would be enough. But there are so many more reasons to be proud of America. Here are just a few:

- We have kept the world free.
- Our system encourages the development of new knowledge and inventions.

- Our sharing of capitalism with the world has made other nations wealthier and freer, including Communist Russia and China.

- We are a very generous nation, annually contributing hundreds of billions to help our own, but also sending huge sums to other countries to help feed and clothe the poor, treat disease, purify the water, and so much more.

- We have opened our doors to people from all over the world and every culture, and once they become U.S. citizens, they are considered Americans.

- Ours is a beautiful country "from the mountains, to the prairies, to the oceans, white with foam ..."

- Our optimistic, entrepreneurial spirit keeps ideas flowing.

- Our system of higher education is the best in the world.

- Our legal system is the most just and fair in the world, built on the priceless concept that a person is innocent until proven guilty.

Our Judeo-Christian Heritage Is a Positive Guiding Force

This doesn't mean that every American should be Jewish or Christian, or that we must all be very religious. And the constitution makes it quite clear that we should not have an official religion, for our founding fathers knew their history and understood the terrible trouble that arises when any religion takes political power.

But there is a difference between separation of church and state, on the one hand, and God and state, on the other. It is God who grants us our rights to life, liberty, and the pursuit of happiness, who insists that we should never bend our knees to tyrants or fanatics of any kind. And by granting these rights to all of us, God tells us that we are all equal before him, and therefore before the law. We have not been granted equality of result; God does not say we must all have exactly the same amount of money, the same beautiful bodies, or the same anything else. But he does insist that we are free and equal in our life, liberty, and pursuit of happiness, and that concept has unleashed the unending waves of energy and creativity that have made this country free and strong.

Our Judeo-Christian heritage is being challenged by multi-culturalism, a destructive idea that encourages us to split ourselves into many different groups, each demanding special recognition and rights from the government. Rather than trusting in the promise of individual rights, they insist on being granted special group rights—such as the right to be ruled by their own religious code instead of our laws—and separating themselves from the mainstream. In essence, they are saying they want to benefit from our laws, our wealth, and the culture that produced that wealth. But at the same time, they don't want anything to do with our laws or what they see as our disgusting culture. They just want to partake in our wealth.

While we are a multicultural society, made up of people from countries all around the world, it is our Judeo-Christian values that made us great. That is why we must nourish and cherish them.

A Strong and Involved U.S. Makes the World a Better Place

The United States rapidly demobilized its armed forces following World War I, and all through the 1920s and 1930s had a very small army and air force. We refused to join the League of Nations, the precursor of the U.N., and felt that what happened "over there" was somebody else's problem.

As we stood back, arms folded, in the 1920s and 1930s, the fascists took control of Italy and the Nazis seized power in Germany. Stalin murdered or starved millions of his own people. The military sized control of Japan, turning that county into a war machine that ravaged China; Spain was torn apart by civil war; Italy invaded Ethiopia. And these were just some of the terrible things that happened while we were weak and uninvolved.

But since the end of World War II, American might has suppressed major wars between major countries, supported the United Nations and many other international organizations, kept the sea lanes open so countries can engage in trade, pushed for colonial powers like England and France to surrender their hold on other peoples, and advocated for free trade that would benefit not just us, but people everywhere. All through the Cold War, our "nuclear umbrella" guaranteed that Western Europe would remain free. And our combined military and economic powers caused the collapse of the Soviet Union, allowing Poland, Hungary, Ukraine, Romania, and many other countries to become free nations.

We must insist on remaining strong—strong enough to support our friends and give our enemies reason to pause.

Some Countries, Cultures and Religions are Good; Others Are Bad

I know it's not politically correct to say this, but there are good countries and bad countries, good cultures and bad cultures, and good religions and bad religions.

Here are a few of the bads:

- Any Communist country is bad. Period. Communism is a morally bankrupt philosophy that has never worked and has always led to loads of problems, ranging from economic hardship to the outright torture and murder of its citizens by the state.

- Any dictatorship is bad. Dictators always give special favors to those who support them and grind the rest under their heels.

- Any country run by religious extremists is bad. Religion can be a force for good, but whenever it's pushed to the extreme, it's bad. Religious extremists stifle and often persecute the "nonbelievers" who live among them, and truly think that anyone who does not believe as they do is evil and must be either converted or destroyed.

- Any religion that tells its followers that they must rid the world of the "nonbelievers" before the Messiah can return or the rapture can occur (or whatever else they want to happen) is bad. This attitude incites hatred and violence.

- Any country or culture that divides people into superior and inferior groups by law or fiat is bad. We're all equal before the Creator, and should be equal in the eyes of the law, with the same right to succeed—or to fail—according to our talents, drive, and luck.

- Any culture or religion that encourages you to "stay in your place" is bad. Everyone should have the right to dream, to strive to improve their circumstances.

As for the "goods," they include any country, culture, or religion that supports democracy, free enterprise, respect for individuality, religious freedom, freedom of speech, and freedom of assembly. They also include those that encourage people to improve themselves and respect the cultures and beliefs of others.

The Government Should Work for the People Only

When I was a boy in Czechoslovakia, I had to step off the sidewalk to make room for any government official coming my way, even if this meant I had to step in the mud. We don't have to yield the sidewalk to government officials in this country, but we have allowed the various levels of government to run amok. They've become a self-perpetuating bureaucracy that is more concerned with keeping its officials employed than doing right by the people.

For example, the executive branch of the federal government has become incredibly bloated, with a staggering number of departments, agencies, bureaus, offices, centers, services, boards, initiatives, administrations, institutes, corps, and other entities. There's a website at usa.gov, which describes itself as the "U.S. government's official web portal." On this website, I found an "A–Z Index of U.S. Government Departments and Agencies," so I decided to count them. There are over 500, which seemed like a lot to me. Then there was another list of "Federal Advisory Committees by Agency" which had over 1,000 names! There was another list of "Quasi-Official Agencies" and one called "Independent Agencies and Government Corporations" and another called "Boards, Commissions and Committees," but I'm ninety-five years old, and I can't waste any more time counting all this nonsense. It's ridiculous! Why do we need all of these people eating up our money and wasting our time?

The federal government has become too big and too convoluted, with too much overreach and overlap between these departments and other units. I don't have a Ph.D. in management, but I'll bet that if you put someone like me in charge, someone who has spent decades running a business in the real world, where pennies count and performance really matters, government could be made lean and efficient. Just large enough to handle its duties, but not so big that it takes something the size of a phone book to list all of its departments, agencies, bureaus, offices, centers, services, boards, initiatives, institutes, administrations, corps, and other entities.

Some people say it's impossible to make the government lean in our complex era. Some people also said it was impossible to send a man to the moon.

We Should Give to Those Unable to Care for Themselves; Everyone Else Should Work!

I was able to escape the Nazis and nearly certain death for one reason: my uncles spent a lot of money bringing their European relatives to America. My American family took me in, fed and clothed me, and treated me as their son. They were very generous to me, to my brother and my sisters, and the many others they rescued.

But the day after I arrived in New York, they put me to work in Uncle Harry's grocery store. Nobody thought this was unusual—in those days it would have been considered strange if I *hadn't* worked. I didn't know the language or the money system or have any of the necessary skills, but there I was earning my keep. It never would have occurred to anyone—including me—to have said, "Oh, let him hang around and do nothing for a couple of years." That idea simply did not exist for us.

But it certainly exists today. Look at how many millions of people have become part of the permanent "welfare class," living off of federal, state, and local programs. Some of these people are truly unable to support themselves; they are elderly or ill, or they are still very young and in school. To them, we should be very generous, making sure that their bellies are full, and that they have a decent place to live, good medical care, and the other necessities of life. It is our duty to take care of them, and they should receive all of these things with nothing expected in return.

Everyone else, however, should be expected to work in exchange for the benefits they receive. Remember, handing people a living without asking for something in return weakens them. When the government gives welfare and other aid with no strings attached, it helps set the recipients up for cycles of poverty that can extend through generations.

Why don't we ask those who receive assistance, and are capable of doing so, to do some work in exchange for what they receive? Not a full week's worth, because they need time to look for a job, but something. They can paint fences, pick up trash in public parks, file papers in the offices of local charities, or something similar. Some people scorn this idea, saying there is no dignity in picking up trash. I say that's ridiculous: *any* honest work is dignified. And how much dignity is there in living off of handouts?

Even if they work only a few days a week in exchange for their benefits, people will enjoy the blessings of work: dignity, a sense of accomplishment, a regular reminder that they are capable, a feeling that they are giving back to their country, and more.

Choose Smaller Government and Return Responsibility to the People

It is necessary to have a strong government that is able to protect its citizens from invasion, fight crime, handle civil disputes, issue and regulate currency, regulate the financial markets, protect free speech and freedom of religion, and set up major organizations such as the Centers for Disease Control. But while a strong government is good, a government that takes on too much can be dangerous.

When our government protects us from foreign invasions and domestic criminals, that's good. But when it tries to protect us from our own actions, when it becomes a scolding nanny, that's bad. For example, do you remember when Michael Bloomberg, the former mayor of New York City, got concerned because so many people in this country are obese? Obesity is a genuine problem, but he wanted to slap a tax on cups of soda sold in New York City that were over a certain size. Cutting back on soda and other fast food is a good idea, but taxing people to save them from their own foolishness is ridiculous. First of all, it doesn't work, because people will always find a way around it. (They could always buy two smaller sodas.) Second, it tells people that they are too silly or too weak to control their eating habits. And finally, it sends the terrible message that only the government knows what's good for you, so you need to do what you're told.

The obesity problem should be tackled at the local level, in schools, churches, and social organizations, through charities and foundations. These groups could raise awareness of the problem, encourage better eating, get exercise programs going, pressure local restaurants and fast-food outlets to offer healthier foods, enlist celebrities in campaigns to make being healthy "cool," and so on. This way, the people themselves could become part of the solution by participating in the various programs and encouraging their children and friends to develop better health habits. Not only does this increase the odds of success, it sends a powerful message: that the people are smart enough to recognize a problem and develop a solution and strong enough to solve it.

I can sum it up like this: our government should have fewer responsibilities and be smaller in size, scope, and budget. It should never act as if it is the people's nanny. As Thomas Jefferson said, "It is to secure our rights that we resort to government at all." Once government secures these rights on our behalf, it should let us citizens take the reins.

A Better America, A Better World

If we take these beliefs to heart, and teach them to our children, the United States will remain strong, and the world will be a better place. Eventually, everyone will enjoy freedom and liberty and will be able to pursue happiness.

CHAPTER THIRTEEN

Beliefs Must Shape Action

It's one thing to have beliefs and take them to heart. But it's quite another to translate these beliefs into concrete action for the good of our families, communities, and country, and that's what is really crucial. How can our beliefs help guide us in setting up our laws and policies? It's really quite simple: Just keep them in mind whenever deciding how to act on an issue.

To see how this plays out, let's take a look at some of our most cherished beliefs to see how they can help us handle major issues facing us today.

Our Judeo-Christian Heritage: How It Affects Religious Displays and Other Issues

Our country does not—and should not—support any religion. Freedom of religion and freedom from persecution due to one's religious beliefs are major tenets of the Constitution; therefore, we must always have a firm separation between church and state. Yet the people of our nation have been guided by certain Judeo-Christian values ever since our forefathers first gathered to talk of throwing off the yoke of foreign oppression. These values can be summarized in three short sentences: We all have free will. We are responsible for ourselves and our actions. We must continually strive to improve ourselves, while taking care of those in genuine need. So even though America does not support any one religion, certain "religious values" are important parts of the foundation of our country.

Unfortunately, some people are opposed to *any* link between religion and state. They have misconstrued the meaning of the First Amendment, which says our government will "make no law respecting an establishment of religion, or prohibiting the free exercise thereof." To them, this means we should wipe out any reference to religion in public buildings and spaces, "cleansing" them of pictures or statues depicting the Ten Commandments or quotes such as "In God We Trust." They want us to remove the words "under God" from the Pledge of Allegiance. These people say that even the slightest reference to Judeo-Christian principles offends people who belong to other faiths, leaving them feeling belittled, ostracized from the community, and fearing they will not receive just treatment at the hands of the law.

Nonsense! These references to God and the basic Judeo-Christian tenets are reminders of our guiding principles. They also remind us that we should treat all of our fellow human beings with love and respect. They do not denigrate any group; in fact, they do just the opposite. If anything, we need *more* of these references, and they should be prominently displayed in public spaces as a celebration of the best parts of humanity and a reminder of our goals.

Being Jewish, I know what it means to be in the religious minority. I remember very well when Jews in this country could not find good jobs in certain industries, belong to various organizations and clubs, or even live in particular neighborhoods. I know what it's like to be stopped dead in my tracks by the unspoken "gentleman's agreement" that politely but firmly turns "my kind" away. I know what it's like to go to public meetings where a minister offers a blessing referring to Jesus Christ, or to walk into a courtroom and see a quote from the New Testament on the wall. But I also understand that the Judeo-Christian values are what made this country great, whether they happen to have originated in my religion or the Christian religion. Stripping symbols of Judeo-Christian values from public buildings, erasing all mention of them from school textbooks, mocking them on television and in print, and using politically correct "thought police" to hound those who support them are just weakening our foundation and ripping us apart. We Americans must continue to hold our Judeo-Christian heritage dear.

As for those who come to this country wishing to become Americans, they must embrace the Judeo-Christian values, as well. It's perfectly fine to be a Buddhist, Muslim, Hindu or anything else and to practice a religion openly and proudly. But—and this is very important—if you want to be an American, you must adopt American values, even if you continue to practice your non-Judeo-Christian religion. You can't come here and say, "My religion demands this and that, and I want it now!" I, as a Jew, can't go to Saudi Arabia, stamp my foot and scream, "My religion demands that you pray to God instead of Allah, change your Sabbath to Saturday, and only serve kosher food in government buildings!" They would laugh me out of town—or throw me in jail.

We can't let other religious groups dictate our government's practices. The most obvious example of this is Muslim women who want to keep their faces covered, even when photographed for a driver's license or other identification papers. What good is an ID picture if a person's face is covered? Do we really want our fear of seeming "unfair" or "prejudiced" push us into ridiculous and, possibly, dangerous policies?

If you want to be an American, show your face on ID photos! When saying the Pledge of Allegiance, don't say "One nation under Allah," say "One nation under God." Don't insist on having "Muslims only" washing areas in universities or public buildings. That's just another form of Jim Crow! (Would you allow "whites only" or "blacks only" washing areas? Or "Jewish only" anything?) If you're a Muslim taxi driver, don't turn away passengers who are carrying alcohol. If you're a Muslim supermarket cashier, don't refuse to sell pork products. We Americans respect your religion and attitudes toward washing, alcohol, dietary restrictions, and other issues in your personal life. But we should never allow you to undermine our core American values. When people ask me what I am, I always say that I am an American Jew. I'm not a Jew who happens to live in America. I'm an *American* who happens to be Jewish—there's a big difference! If people aren't willing to embrace American values, they have no business coming here, except for a visit or a temporary work assignment.

Staying Strong and Involved in World Affairs: How It Affects Homeland Security and Other Issues

One thing is absolutely certain: The United States must remain strong enough to defend democratic capitalism worldwide, or the world will go to hell in a hand basket. This doesn't mean that we have to go to war with every country that disagrees with us. Diplomacy is almost always a better approach, certainly in the beginning stages of a disagreement. However, when it comes to foreign affairs, we should follow Teddy Roosevelt's policy: "Speak softly and carry a big stick."

A strong country has its roots in safety at home. First and foremost, we must protect ourselves against terrorists and other enemies who want to blow up our buildings, shoot down our passenger airplanes, ruin our economy by hacking into our banks and stock market, and so on. This, unfortunately, requires a powerful Department of Homeland Security, backed by legislation allowing it to spy on enemies in our country and arrest them when necessary. In order to grant this kind of power, the government must become more flexible about protecting our civil rights, and may need to engage in unpleasant activities like reading emails and tapping phones more often than we might like. Naturally, there must be strong suspicions to justify this sort of behavior, and the government should never overstep legal boundaries. But sometimes it's necessary to give up a certain amount of personal privacy in the name of national security.

This idea is often disturbing to Americans, who prize their liberty and privacy, but it's the price we must pay to remain strong and free. In days past, it was difficult for our enemies to attack us where we live. Today, it's much easier for them to sneak into the country, live among us, ship in dangerous weapons, use the Internet to communicate with each other, and plot against us. To protect ourselves and to catch these people before they do any harm, we must be willing to sacrifice some of our own liberty. That being said, the activities of the Department of Homeland Security should be continually monitored by the Senate and House committees to make sure no one steps over the line. And laws that allow such activities should be limited by "sunset" provisions that require re-approval every few years.

One key part of domestic security is securing our borders, something that is notoriously lacking at present. We must lock down our borders *now*, so no one else can get in without our knowledge and approval. Many people are against this, as it will prevent millions of people from sneaking into our country to live and work. But let me be very clear about this: *Illegal* immigration is bad, and illegal immigrants have no right to be here. They broke our laws when they came here without permission and they continue to break our laws by remaining. And notice that I say "illegal immigrants." I am very much against calling these people "undocumented workers," as it's a way of whitewashing their illegal activities. This label makes it sound as if they just have some little problem with their immigration papers. Yes, there's a problem: they don't have any papers! They are illegal aliens and should be treated as such.

I believe that anyone who wants to come to America should do what I did: apply for and receive permission from the government to live here and become a citizen. And we legal Americans should retain the right to throw out anyone who does not have permission—immediately!

The illegal immigrant problem has become so overwhelming because we never spent the time or money it takes to lock down our borders. We need to build physical walls, set up "radar walls," patrol the borders with immigration personnel and drones, and do whatever else it takes to make sure that no one else can sneak in. The problem is not going away if we ignore it; it's only going to get worse.

We must also require—even demand!—that all illegal aliens immediately register with the government. This should be coupled with employment regulations and other rules that make it very difficult for anyone to remain hidden. And once these people have registered, they should be checked out very carefully. If they've lived here for, let's say, ten years and have a perfectly clean record, they should be put on a path to citizenship. Not *handed* citizenship, but allowed to begin a lengthy and difficult process that includes studying English, learning our history and, most importantly, understanding what America stands for and what it means to be an American.

I know that some people will say that it's unfair that illegal aliens should have to work so hard to become citizens. But it is not a matter of fairness: it's what is *right*. They should have to work hard to demonstrate their willingness to become one of us. I went to night school to learn English, after putting in long hours of work during the day. It wasn't easy, but it never would have occurred to me to ask for anything different.

Any illegal immigrants who have not lived here for a specific length of time or do not have a clean record should be shipped out—no ifs, ands or buts. And if that means separating a family, say, tossing out a parent who has engaged in criminal activity, that's too bad. If the family wants to stay together, the other family members are free to leave along with the criminal. Would this be hard on the innocent children of the criminal? You bet. But who caused this terrible situation? If anyone was unfair or at fault, it was the criminal.

Besides securing our borders and putting worthy illegal aliens on a path to citizenship, we need to change our relationship with the United Nations. In theory, the U.N. is a great idea, a place for the nations of the world to gather to discuss and settle their disputes. In reality, it's become a baseball bat used to beat the United States over the head. Some countries try to use the U.N. to condemn and block our actions, while others want us to subordinate our interests to the "world community" (translation: to grant the U.N. the power to use our economic and military power as it sees fit). Either way, whether we're blocked or subordinated, we lose. That's why we should never put our armed forces under the command of the U.N. or any other such "world community" organization. These organizations are either opposed to what we stand for or too eager to spend our blood and money in pursuit of their own goals. We need to change our relationship with the U.N., and only participate in activities like helping countries hit by natural disasters or negotiating international treaties regarding business, postage delivery, and similar issues.

Finally, to remain strong, we must keep up the battle against militant Islamists, terrorists, and all others who wish to harm us. Militant Islamists fiercely oppose our ideas and way of life. They believe that we stand in the way of spreading of their destructive philosophy throughout the world, and their ultimate goal is our destruction. Like the Communists before them, the militant

Islamists must be opposed and kept in check until, by their own rotten accord, they self-destruct.

But deciding how to oppose militant Islamists and others who wish to harm us is a tricky matter. Our choices are diplomacy, economic pressure, indirect military support (such as supplying rebels), military engagement via drones, and close-up military engagement with "boots on the ground." Finding the best combination is difficult, and sometimes we won't get it right. We made mistakes fighting the Nazis and the Japanese during World War II, and made others when combating Communism in the decades that followed. We also made some bad decisions in Iraq and Afghanistan. We've learned, for example, that we can't just knock off an evil dictator and say to his people, "You're free now. Have some elections, set up independent courts, open your businesses, and everything will be fine." Freedom, democracy, and capitalism are strange new ideas in many countries and difficult to put into play. It will take years of working with the new leaders of these countries to help them wean their people from the old ways and slowly establish a democratic way of life. Mistakes are always painful, so we should continually reassess our political and military strategies. But we *must* stay the course! Every time we support freedom, every time we strengthen democratic capitalism, we make the world a better place.

Our resolve to do difficult things like this has wavered over the past several decades. That's not surprising, for our citizens no longer seem to know what this country stands for. Our children are not taught nearly enough American history during their school years, and many college students take absolutely no history classes: of the top fifty public universities in this country, only five require students to take even one course in American history!

Several years ago, students at universities across the country were given a civics literacy test, with questions concerning American history and government, international affairs, and the market economy. The results were dismal. Less than half of college seniors knew that NATO had been formed to protect Western Europe from an aggressive Soviet Union, or that the British were defeated at the battle of Yorktown, which ended the American Revolutionary War. The average score on the test was 50.4 percent for freshmen and 54.2 percent for seniors—both of which translate to a grade of "F." The situation was even worse among younger students, with less than 25 percent of elementary and high school students qualifying as "proficient" in American history.

The lack of American history in school and college curriculums is only the beginning. Most of the history that *is* taught is often presented in a very anti-American manner. How can you grow to love your country when you are constantly told how bad it is? While we don't want to whitewash our mistakes, we certainly shouldn't tar and feather our country!

I believe that children should study American history every year from kindergarten straight through college, with the course content proudly emphasizing the strength and beauty of America. And when teachers explore our country's mistakes and examine alternative political/economic systems such as Communism, these topics should be presented in a neutral manner that allows students to draw their own conclusions.

I am also a firm believer in eliminating tenure for college professors. What may have initially been a good idea has long been abused, with left-wing radicals seizing control of history, political science, and other departments in colleges and universities across the country. For these radicals, history and political science are no longer subjects to be taught; they are a means of instilling disgust for this country in the students. Protected by lifetime employment, they are poisoning the minds of our young people, and in so doing, poisoning our future. And since the already-tenured professors have the right to veto new applicants, they make sure that tenure is granted only to new professors who think exactly as they do. In essence, they accept only clones of themselves, guaranteeing that radical left-wing professors will continue to ruin young minds for decades to come.

Tenured professors spend too much time researching and writing articles and books critical of this country and its beliefs. They are hardly required to spend any time in the classroom, for most of the teaching is left to adjunct professors and teaching assistants who can be fired at will, no matter how wonderful their teaching skills may be, and no matter how much their students learn. Meanwhile, the tenured professors are paid much, much more than the "lower" teachers, many of whom rush from college to college teaching a class here and a class there, trying desperately to earn enough to stay alive.

Besides the other problems with tenure, it allows those who have it to grow fat and lazy, for once they are tenured it is nearly impossible to get rid of them. It's time to eliminate tenure. *All* professors should be forced to defend and justify what they teach, why they teach it, and how they teach it, and not be allowed to hide behind these harmful lifetime contracts.

A Government That Works for the People: How It Affects Big Government, Affirmative Action, and Other Issues

Our government today has become so large that it no longer works for the people. It works for itself and is run by career politicians whose primary interest is getting re-elected. It is a self-perpetuating bureaucracy with the major goals of staying alive, assuring a steady influx of money, and keeping employees on the payroll. These goals might be fine if the government was a factory that actually produced something. But it doesn't produce anything other than legislation. A nation prospers when it grows food, manufactures products, builds houses, and so on, but our government doesn't do any of this. Yet there are over 20 million people on today's federal, state, and local government payrolls— almost twice as many as the combined number of those employed in the manufacturing, farming, fishing, mining, utilities, and construction industries. This overload of government employees has resulted in the micromanaging of businesses and the creation and enforcement of endless rules.

We certainly need government to develop and enforce safety standards, test and license professionals, set and maintain the laws and contracts necessary for public safety and the smooth running of business, protect American industry from unfair foreign competition, and so on. But today there are just too many rules for employers and employees to follow. These rules micromanage the workers and require companies to hire hordes of accountants, lawyers, and "compliance officers" to make sure every bureaucratic "i" is dotted and every "t" crossed. This stifles both production and creativity, and the costs to business are astronomical. The government is certainly *not* working in the best interests of the people in this case. What we need is smaller government and less interference in business and industry. Today's Big Brother approach is just getting in the way.

To help ensure the government is truly connected to the people, we should prevent senators, congressmen, and others from growing fat and lazy in their jobs and rousing themselves only when it's time to raise more money or get re-elected. The best way to do this is through term limits. The numbers can certainly be debated, but I think that a maximum of ten years in the U.S. Senate and House of Representatives combined is plenty. Limits like these will ensure that new citizens constantly flow through the Senate and House, bringing new perspectives and ideas. It's not a perfect solution, but it's a way to get some fresh blood into what are often compromised, over-privileged, and abused governmental positions. We need "citizen legislators" with genuine, hard-won experience in the real world, people who have built houses or flipped burgers with their own hands, who have created companies or new concepts, who have been forced to cut way back during bad economic times, who have been forced to face the wrath of angry customers up close and personal, who have otherwise lived in the real world, and who are willing to give this country the benefit of their hard-won wisdom—but only for a few years. Anybody who wants to remain in government for longer than that should be considered suspect. And I mean *very* suspect. After all, our Congress is stuffed full of career politicians, and most of our national, state, and local leaders are career politicians. These are the same folks who get us into one financial or foreign policy or social policy mess after another. They are the same ones who run the Bureau of Veterans Affairs or IRS or local sheriff's department and other institutions that are repeatedly failing or being used to fulfill someone's political agenda or to go after somebody's political opponents. We need non-career politicians, talented and dedicated people who understand the real world and are willing to go to Washington just long enough to help out—and then get out!

Another way that the government works against the people is by relentlessly pushing for affirmative action. This country was certainly racially divided when I arrived, back in the 1930s. No question about it, the blacks (among other groups) were treated very cruelly, forced by laws and customs to live apart from the whites, held back economically and educationally, and often prevented from voting. It was a *shanda* (a shame), as my father would have said. Luckily, many brave people fought for civil rights for all citizens, and today we have a truly free and equal society. But you'd never know it if you listened to people like Jesse Jackson or Al Sharpton, who constantly fan the flames of hatred by harping about what a miserable, racist country this is.

I don't agree with this stance. But I do agree that the question that underlies it is an important one for all racial and socioeconomic groups: How can we help ensure that *all* Americans have the opportunity to thrive? The government thinks one answer is to use affirmative action to provide special opportunities to certain minority groups considered to be disadvantaged and/or discriminated against. Affirmative action made sense decades ago, when many minority groups were desperately trying to claw their way out of an oppressive system.

But that's all changed today; the playing field has been leveled. Over the past fifty years, the rate of poverty among blacks has fallen, while the percentage of young blacks attending college has risen dramatically. Today, the sitting President of the United States and the Attorney General are black. Four members of President George W. Bush's cabinet were black, as were seven members of President Bill Clinton's. Blacks are serving, or have served, as CEOs or chairs of the board of major corporations such as Microsoft Crop, Merck & Co., American Express, McDonald's, and Xerox. Incredibly talented blacks such as Oprah Winfrey and Robert Johnson (founder of Black Entertainment Television, or BET) have profoundly influenced our culture and society. Although we need to go further to close gaps between blacks and whites in income levels, health status, rates of incarceration, and other areas, blacks are as viable a group of citizens as any other.

Thus, it's an outrageous affront to blacks and other minorities to give them an automatic "leg up" through affirmative action, allowing black students admission to top universities even when their test scores are low, insisting that businesses hire a certain "quota" from "minority" groups, and so on. It's a blatant message to minorities that they still can't make it on their own. It infantilizes them, metaphorically patting them on the head and saying, "Don't worry, you helpless creatures. I'll take good care of you."

And what of the people who are not minorities? Is it right for those who are well qualified for certain jobs or acceptance to

colleges or universities to be kicked aside so that those less qualified can fill a quota? What happened to the assertion found in the
Declaration of Independence that "all men are created equal"?

The minorities don't need special breaks from the government in order to succeed. I was born a very poor Jew in
Czechoslovakia, a country in which anti-Semitism was rampant
and people made no bones about their disgust for me and my kind.
For hundreds of years before, Jews had been persecuted and mas-
sacred throughout Europe, and the Holocaust was only a few years
away. There was no affirmative action plan helping me out, and
yet I made it anyway. For that, in part, I have my mother to thank.
She prepared me to succeed in an oppressive society by teaching
me the following lessons:

- Study hard in school and get all the experience you can in the
  "school of hard knocks."

- Work as hard and smart as you can.

- Steel yourself against small-minded people who stand in your
  way.

- Always maintain your dignity, no matter what people throw
  at you.

- Keep your goals firmly in mind.

- Keep pushing through.

- Show your best face to the non-Jews.

- Once you've succeeded, become a role model to all young Jews.

It's a recipe for success that can translate to any group.

Here in America, if you experience injustice or feel that you are being held back due to prejudice, you have options. You can protest (peacefully!) in the streets, pressure the company that behaved badly with boycotts and other means, sue them, and use all the other tools built into our capitalist democracy. Dollars and votes can also be powerful weapons, when you use them wisely.

Giving Generously to Those in Need: How It Affects Welfare and Other Issues

President Lyndon Johnson launched the "War on Poverty" half a century ago, his stated goal being "not only to relieve the symptom of poverty, but to cure it and, above all, to prevent it." Since that time, we've spent over *$20 trillion* on welfare and other programs for the poor. Yet poverty remains a pressing problem to this day.

There's no doubt that there are still too many people who go to bed hungry, and we must do more to help them. Those who are genuinely unable to work or care for themselves should be well taken care of by society. But by and large, the poor in America are *not* starving beggars dressed in rags. The federal government spends a little over $20,000 a year per poor person, or $60,000 for a family of three. If money alone were the solution, poverty would have been wiped out a long time ago. Yet the poverty rate has remained fairly stable, at about 15 percent, since the War on Poverty began.

Obviously, the poor are not suffering from a lack of aid. They are suffering from a poverty of possibility. They simply don't believe that they can improve their lives through hard work and determination, along with just enough assistance to get started.

A major reason that so many of the poor suffer a poverty of possibility is that they are dazzled by the endless array of government handouts. Poor people are not fools; they respond to incentives just like everyone else. They see how much easier it is to accept handouts than to work in an entry-level job. And since the human brain cannot focus on opposing ideas at the same time, the poor *cannot* see the possibility of doing better.

What the vast majority of poor people desperately need is *less* welfare. Instead, if they are of sound mind and body, the best "medicine" for them is steady work. If the government really wants to assist, it must stop the endless giveaways. Welfare programs must be revamped, offering *temporary* assistance that is specifically geared toward helping people get back on their feet and back to work.

To do so, the government must first determine how much money it is giving away, to whom, and why. A few years ago, a committee from the House of Representatives held a hearing called "Duplication, Overlap, and Inefficiencies in Federal Welfare Programs." Patricia Dalton, of the government's General Accountability Office (GAO), testified that the GAO had *no idea* how many welfare programs were in operation or how much was being spent. She also said the GAO couldn't even "hazard a guess" as to how many of those programs were achieving their goals.

This is insanity! If a business operated this way, it would go broke and be swept away in short order, or be forced to completely refashion its methods of operation. Why shouldn't government be required to function the same way?

There must be a clear accounting of what is being spent, who is receiving assistance, and why. And then the cutbacks must begin. All welfare recipients who are able to work should be informed that their payments will be tapered off and disappear after a certain date. If they can't find a job by then, they must report to a work center every day, where they will be assigned tasks like cleaning up public parks and assisting local charities. People who are able-bodied and receiving money from the government should be required to work for it—with time off to go to job interviews, of course.

Of course this idea doesn't work well if there are no jobs available, and the lack of jobs is a currently a big problem in our country. To improve the job market, the government needs to make it easier for employers to hire people. Employers struggle with a never-ending barrage of rules, regulations, and taxes that make it difficult to take on employees. They worry about being hit with fines for failing to comply with endless, obscure employment rules. There is always the possibility of lawsuits over discrimination, sexual harassment, and more. Obamacare has added even more red tape. Large employers can set up human resources departments that have clever lawyers who can deal with all this nonsense. But most businesses are not very large, which means that the owners themselves must constantly try to handle these difficult issues—and they often fail because the rules are so complex. I've met many small business owners who tell me they absolutely refuse to hire any more people. One man, whose company had nineteen employees, was dead set against hiring even one more person because twenty employees was considered a "big" company in his state, and he would then have to comply with a whole new set of employment rules.

This country has sent men to the moon. Surely we can figure out a way to take an accurate accounting of the welfare we're doling out, streamline the system, ensure that only those in genuine need are given assistance, and give the rest of the people a strong incentive to work. And surely we can change our employment rules so that employers are encouraged to hire our own citizens, rather than illegals. But we will have to be willing to make some radical changes.

Always Choose Smaller Government: How This Affects Income Tax, Health Care, and Other Issues

Once the federal government is large enough and strong enough to fulfill its essential functions (including developing a strong military force, regulating the currency, and securing the rights of the citizens), we citizens should be very wary of allowing it to grow any larger. Large governments are, by nature, unaccountable and inefficient.

You'd think that the more people there are, the greater the likelihood that a given job will be done well. After all, there's plenty of talent and energy to go around. But it's not so in a large government. With hundreds of departments and agencies, each supporting hundreds or even thousands of employees, it's almost impossible to hold any one person accountable for anything—especially when many of these agencies have overlapping functions.

And this means there's a lot less incentive for any one employee to do a good job. After all, any failures probably won't be traced back to him or her. Generally, government employees just want to hang on to their jobs; doing excellent work and going that extra mile is not part of the game plan. And adding more employees, more committees, and more departments doesn't improve governmental efficiency; if anything, it degrades it.

That's why once the basic functions are taken care of, the federal government should be prevented from growing larger. Whenever possible, we should take away excess responsibilities from the federal government and return them to the states, or even to the counties and cities. It's much easier to figure out what these smaller governmental units are doing and hold them responsible for their actions. Although shrinking the federal government will be tough because entrenched bureaucrats will fight tooth and nail to protect their jobs, we must do it.

There are many ways to shrink the federal government, chief of which is simplifying income tax. Throw out the federal income tax code, which is so overgrown that the U.S. Tax Code is 73,000 pages long! This convoluted and confusing code forces businesses and individuals to waste an incredible amount of time keeping track of all the rules. It also guarantees lifetime employment for IRS bureaucrats, encourages large businesses to re-incorporate overseas, and forces all business to think about the tax consequences of taking any kind of action—when they really should be thinking about the business consequences. It's time to replace our current income tax disaster with a flat tax.

The idea is very simple: everyone pays a certain percentage, say 10 percent, of their income every year. There are no deductions. There is no "marriage penalty," no double taxation for dividends or earned income credit, and no other tax games. Everybody pays the same rate. This is perfectly fair because the more money a person earns, the more he pays: a millionaire will pay much more than a middle-class earner. As for low-income workers, by insisting that they, too, pay tax, we make them part of the system. Since everyone will be contributing, everyone will have an interest in keeping the government from taking too much away from them.

There are other benefits to the flat tax, including cutting the overblown IRS down to a very small size, and making it absolutely clear to each of us how much we are sending to Uncle Sam every year. If that 10 percent goes up, even if only to 11 percent, it will be obvious to all, and the government will have to justify it to a lot of angry people. This, in turn, will make it harder for the government to become overgrown. An additional advantage: with a flat tax, there is no chance the president can use the IRS to attack or hinder his opponents.

Another way to keep the federal government small is to remove it from the health care business. For decades, the federal government has been operating the Veterans Administration (VA), a national health care system designed for those who have served in the military. Although limited in the sense that it's only for veterans, the VA is nonetheless a national health care system, one that is very similar to those seen in England, Sweden, and other countries. It's also an ongoing disaster. In the latest of many scandals, VA officials were caught falsifying data so they could pretend they were treating their patients in a timely manner. What they were really doing was sending many of the patients home before they had received proper care, and hundreds died as a result. Even President Obama had to admit that the situation was disgraceful. And this was not a one-time problem, as the VA has been plagued by inefficiency and poor care practically from the beginning.

The federal government also operates a second national health care system called Medicare, which pays for and regulates the health care of seniors and certain other groups. The program may be well-intended, but the government has promised care to so many people that it can't afford to pay for it all. As a result, it is paying doctors so little that many of them don't want to treat Medicare patients. Or they run them through their offices as rapidly as possible so the high volume will bring in enough money to cover their expenses. Doctors, hospitals, and other health care providers also try to make up for it by charging more to patients with other forms of insurance, and even more to those who pay cash.

Yet despite the fact that the federal government has *proven* it cannot operate a national health care system, it has launched a massive new health care system, commonly called Obamacare. And the problems already seem insurmountable. Not only was the Obamacare rollout a total disaster, the government is now forcing more and more businesses to offer health care to their full-time employees. As a result, many firms have cut back on workers' hours, keeping them in the "part time" category so the company won't have to provide insurance. Businesses should be in the business of *business*, not in the business of health care.

I firmly believe that the federal government should get out of health care altogether. Health care is best handled by the private sector, using a system in which people compensate their doctors with a combination of insurance payments and their own money. I believe that when people contribute some of their own hard-earned money to their health care they will question their doctors more carefully about the treatment, and find out if they really need it. The doctors will know that they need to keep their patients satisfied and in good health or they'll go elsewhere. A major factor in the big run-up of health costs was overreliance on governmental and private insurance payments. Patients didn't balk, because the money wasn't coming out of their pockets, so the health care industry tended to over-treat illnesses and overcharge for everything. As time went by, prices continued to skyrocket.

Insurance should function as a backup for the treatment of major health problems, not a free bank. The federal government's role should be to monitor the doctors, hospitals, and other health providers to make sure they are qualified and performing well. It should also regulate the health insurance companies to make sure they fulfill *all* of their promises, pay claims promptly and properly, and otherwise operate strictly according to the rules.

Follow the Beliefs

Political, economic, and moral issues can be complex and difficult to understand. But I have found that whenever an issue arises, if I think about my core beliefs, I can find the guidance I need to make the right choice.

If I leave you with one thing, if you forget all of my stories and opinions, I hope you will remember these important ideas:

- The United States is a wonderful country, with a rich history and culture and a long list of accomplishments. Admire and respect other nations and peoples, but love the U.S.A.!

- Our Judeo-Christian heritage has been a positive guiding force that must be nourished and cherished.

- As long as the U.S. remains strong and involved in world affairs, the world will be an increasingly better place.

- Some countries, cultures, and/or religions are good, while others are bad.

- Our government should always and only work for the people.

- We must give generously to those who are genuinely unable to care for themselves—but everyone else must work.

- When given a choice between smaller and larger government, smaller government, which returns responsibility to the people, is always the better choice.

As long as we keep these ideas alive in our hearts and minds, America will continue to be a wonderful country that encourages freedom, opportunity, and prosperity throughout the world.

America, I love you!

AFTERWORD

A lot has happened in the world during the months I spent writing this book; so much so that I am astounded. It often seems like mankind is regressing, rather than progressing.

ISIS, the barbaric "Islamic State of Iraq and Syria," is presently slaughtering its way through Syria and Iraq, beheading kidnapped Western journalists, aid workers, and tourists, even chopping off the heads of fellow Arabs because they dare to be Christian. ISIS's goal is to establish a radical Islamic caliphate in the Middle East led by a supreme religious and political leader, forcing everyone to accept a violent and oppressive religion—at the point of a sword if need be. In Australia, police thwarted an ISIS plot to "conduct demonstration killings here in this country." Beheadings, "demonstration killings"? Is this the new norm?

Meanwhile, Russia has dropped all pretense of being part of the community of nations in its drive to take over neighboring Ukraine, and Libya has become a failed state, prey to the numerous warlords who have violently staked out territories, and the parade of horribles continues.

And we're not without our problems here in the U.S. The great American dream of owning a home is fading fast for our young people. This is largely the result of the skyrocketing cost of higher education, which forces students to borrow so much money that they're too saddled with debt to qualify for a home loan once they graduate and begin working. Buying a home is an important way for the average person to accumulate wealth, so fencing so many of our young people out of the real estate market does not bode well for our national economic future.

And it's not just our financial future that appears to be in trouble. Our physical safety is also at increasing risk. Bomb threats, school shootings, and other horrors have become routine. The FBI has just released a study noting that "The number of incidents in which a shooter opens fire on a crowd of people more than doubled over the past seven years compared with the previous seven ..."

Then there's the continuing insanity regarding the treatment of illegal immigrants, people who break the law every day simply by being here. The state of California is preparing to hand out driver's licenses to over one million illegal immigrants. After just barely emerging from a long period of financial distress, California will spend $141 million over the next three years to produce and distribute licenses to people who openly flout our laws!

The list of problems could go on and on, but they all point to the fact that we've lost belief in our nation and faith in what it stands for. And we've lost belief in our future. A new poll conducted by the *Wall Street Journal* and NBC News asked Americans whether "life for our children's generation will be better than it has been for us." The results, reported in the *Washington Post*, were shocking: an incredible 76 percent said no, the future will *not* be better! These grim results occurred across the board, in Democrats and

Republicans, men and women, young and old, and all races. As the *Washington Post* pointed out, "This fractious nation is united by one thing: lost faith in the United States."

This country was founded on the belief in a better future, and for over 200 years we've thrived and made the world better because of that belief. But now it's fading away.

Who will lead us out of our malaise? Where are great leaders, people like George Washington and Abraham Lincoln and Martin Luther King, who are willing to stand up for what is right? Who can inspire us to dream, to reach for the stars? True leaders are few and far between today, and it's no wonder. When the country has lost belief in itself, it is difficult to find leaders who care about anything more than the next election.

I can't tell you exactly which ideas will make our economy catch fire, which foreign policy paths to follow, or how to rebuild our highways and other infrastructure. But of this, I am sure: We *must* recover our beliefs in ourselves and our country. And when we do, our collective path will become much clearer and the future much brighter.